The Search for Mear

The Search for Meaning

A Journey Through World Spiritual Traditions and Practices

Elena Ray

Mindful Pages

Published in 2024

ISBN: 9789358811896 (PB)
ISBN: 9789358811384 (eBook)

Published by

Mindful Pages
Imprint of Alpha Editions LLC
312 W. 2nd St #1834
Casper, WY 82601, USA
www.mindfulpagespublishers.com

Contents

Introduction 1

Part I: Foundations of Spiritualism 7

Chapter 1: The Essence of Spirituality 9

Chapter 2: Historical Overview of Spiritual Traditions 16

Part II: Diverse Spiritual Paths 29

Chapter 3: Eastern Traditions 31

Chapter 4: Western Traditions 49

Chapter 5: Indigenous and Pagan Traditions 62

Chapter 6: New Age and Hybrid Spiritual Movements 77

Part III: Practices and Rituals 91

Chapter 7: Spiritual Practices 93

Chapter 8: Sacred Rituals and Ceremonies 106

Part IV: Spiritual Paths to Personal Growth 119

Chapter 9: Overcoming Challenges Through Spirituality 121

Chapter 10: Ethics and Morality in Spiritual Life 132

Chapter 11: Exploring Your Spiritual Identity 146

Chapter 12: Integrating Spirituality into Everyday Life 157

About the Author 164

Introduction

In every corner of the world and every epoch of history, human beings have embarked on quests to understand the deeper meanings of existence. This universal journey transcends geographical and cultural boundaries, uniting us in our shared search for spiritual understanding. "The Search for Meaning: A Journey Through World Spiritual Traditions and Practices" aims to explore this vast landscape of spiritual inquiry, offering a window into the rich variety of ways humans have sought connection, purpose, and enlightenment.

From the ancient shamanistic rituals of the Siberian tundra to the sophisticated philosophical inquiries of Classical Greece, from the meditative practices of Buddhist monks in the Himalayas to the prayer rituals of the Abrahamic faiths in deserts and bustling cities alike, spirituality forms an integral part of our global heritage. Each tradition provides unique insights into the spiritual dimensions of life, offering paths to personal transformation and collective understanding.

This book is not just a compilation of spiritual ideologies; it is an invitation to explore the diverse spiritual paths that people around the world have walked in their quest for meaning. By journeying through various beliefs and practices, from the most ancient to those of the modern era, we aim to build bridges of understanding and appreciation across different cultures and spiritual ideologies.

As we delve into the essence of spirituality, distinguishing it from organized religion, we uncover the personal, often intimate, practices that support individuals in making sense of their lives and their connections to the world around them. This exploration is not just academic but a call to introspection and discovery. Whether you are a novice to spiritual concepts or someone with substantial experience in spiritual practices, this book offers a comprehensive guide through the myriad ways humans have sought and found meaning in their lives.

By the end of this journey, we hope to have provided a detailed account of world spiritual traditions and practices and enriched your understanding of how spirituality can infuse our daily lives with more profound significance and joy. This exploration is about opening doors, challenging preconceptions, and embracing the richness of the human spirit in its quest for the eternal and the profound.

An Overview of Spiritualism

In today's rapidly changing world, the search for personal peace and deeper meaning remains more relevant than ever. Spiritualism, often misunderstood as merely a form of religious expression, is a broader and more inclusive concept encompassing various beliefs and practices aimed at understanding the inner self and its connection to the universe. This article delves into the essence of spiritualism, exploring its foundations, expressions, and role in contemporary life.

At its core, spiritualism refers to a belief in the non-material aspects of life — the idea that our existence is not limited to physical realities but includes spiritual or metaphysical dimensions. It centers on the belief that life extends beyond what we perceive with our senses, advocating for a connection with something greater than ourselves, whether one defines that as a divine presence, universal energy, or simply a deeper sense of self-awareness.

The roots of spiritualism can be traced back to ancient civilizations, where it often intertwined with religious rituals and the worship of deities. However, the modern spiritualist movement began in the mid-19th century, marked by an increased interest in the paranormal, including communication with the dead. It was a period characterized by rapid scientific discovery and the questioning of traditional religious doctrines, leading to a new framework for exploring the intersection of science, philosophy, and spirituality.

In contemporary settings, spiritualism has evolved to include many practices and beliefs, from traditional mediums and séances to more personal, introspective practices like meditation, mindfulness, and yoga. These practices share a common goal: to help individuals achieve harmony and understanding about their place in the universe.

One of the most appealing aspects of spiritualism is its accessibility. Unlike many organized religions that require adherence to specific doctrines, spiritualism allows individuals to explore their spirituality in a manner that suits their personal beliefs and experiences. This flexibility has contributed to its growing popularity, particularly among those who feel disconnected from traditional religious institutions.

Today, many people incorporate spiritualist practices into their daily routines to promote mental and emotional well-being. For example, meditation and mindfulness can reduce stress, enhance concentration, and improve overall health. Similarly, journaling or engaging in spiritual retreats can provide deeper insights into personal challenges and successes, fostering a greater sense of peace and purpose.

Despite its benefits, spiritualism is not without its critics. Skeptics argue that some aspects of spiritualism lack empirical support and can lead to exploitation, particularly in the realm of mediumship and psychic readings. Furthermore, the broad and often vague nature of spiritualism can lead to inconsistencies and confusion about what it truly means to be a spiritualist.

Spiritualism offers a unique and flexible path for personal exploration and understanding, appealing to those seeking to deepen their connection to the world around them without the confines of structured religion. As society continues to evolve, the principles of spiritualism—self-awareness, harmony, and a deeper understanding of the universe—remain as relevant as ever, providing a supportive foundation for individuals navigating the complexities of modern life.

In its essence, spiritualism encourages us to look within and beyond, to live in harmony with the universe and ourselves, fostering a spiritually fulfilling and meaningful life.

The Universal Quest for Meaning

Throughout human history, every culture and society has a common thread—an innate desire to find purpose and meaning in life. This universal quest is not just a philosophical or religious endeavor; it is deeply embedded in our human psyche, influencing how we shape our identities, make decisions, and perceive the world around us. This article explores the reasons behind this universal quest and examines its implications for individuals and societies.

At its heart, the quest for meaning is driven by the need to make sense of our existence. Psychological theories suggest that having a purpose serves as a crucial anchor, giving direction and motivation to our actions. Viktor Frankl, an Austrian neurologist, psychiatrist, Holocaust survivor, and author of "Man's Search for Meaning," proposed that the primary drive in human beings is not pleasure (as Freud suggested) or power (as Adler suggested), but a pursuit of what he called "meaning." According to Frankl, when individuals find meaning in their suffering, they are more resilient and capable of overcoming adversities.

This quest for meaning transcends individual experiences, reaching into the cultural and spiritual domains. Different cultures have evolved unique spiritual and philosophical systems to provide frameworks within which individuals can find meaning. For instance, in many Eastern traditions like Buddhism and Hinduism, the search for meaning often involves attaining higher awareness or enlightenment. In contrast, Western philosophies might focus more on individualism and the pursuit of personal goals as a source of meaning.

The collective pursuit of meaning also has profound societal implications. Societies that nurture a sense of purpose and community tend to have lower mental health issues, higher productivity, and more cohesive social structures. Conversely, a lack of collective meaning can lead to social unrest, existential angst, and a decline in overall well-being.

The quest for meaning has become more complex and urgent in our modern world. The rapid pace of technological change, the pervasiveness of social media, and the shifting socio-economic landscapes have left many feeling disconnected and disillusioned. The materialistic focus of much of contemporary life often leads to a 'meaning crisis' where individuals feel a lack of connection to something greater than themselves.

Despite these challenges, or perhaps because of them, many are now returning to old and new ways of meaning-making. Some find purpose through reconnecting with nature, engaging in community service, or pursuing creative endeavors. Others explore traditional spiritual paths or adopt new-age spiritual practices. Importantly, the internet has democratized access to many philosophical and spiritual resources, enabling a global exchange of ideas about what it means to lead a meaningful life.

The universal quest for meaning is as relevant today as ever. It is a journey that can profoundly impact personal happiness and societal well-being. While the paths to finding meaning may vary greatly across different cultures and individual experiences, the pursuit itself highlights a shared aspect of human existence—the desire to understand our place in the world and to live lives filled with purpose. In embracing this quest, we enrich our lives and contribute to a more thoughtful, compassionate, and connected world.

Part I: Foundations of Spiritualism

Chapter 1: The Essence of Spirituality

Defining spirituality often evokes a spectrum of descriptions, interpretations, and practices, distinct in their form yet converging in their quest for an intimate understanding of life's essence. As we elucidate the contours of spirituality, it becomes imperative to appreciate its expansive scope and intrinsic divergence from traditional religious frameworks. Spirituality is deeply personal, fluid in nature, and lacks a rigid doctrinal base, which sets it markedly apart from more structured religious systems that often operate within a defined set of beliefs and practices sanctioned by specific institutions.

Spirituality, in its essence, transcends the confines of religious dogma to embrace a more inclusive and individualistic approach. It is a broad domain that encompasses personal growth, a profound connection with the transcendent, and an enduring pursuit of inner peace. While these elements are also sometimes part of religious experience, spirituality does not demand conformity to an external set of rules but rather encourages an internal exploration aimed at personal enlightenment and understanding.

The personal growth aspect of spirituality is multifaceted, involving emotional, mental, and sometimes physical developments that contribute to the maturation of the individual spirit. For many, this path includes practices such as meditation, contemplative prayer, or yoga, which provide tools for self-discipline, increased awareness, and a deeper connection with oneself. These practices are often pursued with the goal of achieving a state of harmony within oneself and with the surrounding world, enhancing one's resilience against the vicissitudes of life.

Connection with the transcendent is another crucial dimension of spirituality. This transcendence can be conceptualised as connecting with a reality that is greater than oneself and can be understood as divine, cosmic, or merely as the profound interconnectivity of all life. Such a connection often involves awe and wonder at something vastly beyond one's personal experience and can lead to significant shifts in perspective and life understanding. It allows individuals to step beyond the ego-driven confines of their existence, fostering a sense of belonging and universality.

Pursuing inner peace, a core endeavour of many spiritual practices, involves finding ways to live in equanimity amidst the often chaotic environments of modern life. Achieving this state can mean different things to different people; however, it generally involves a sense of stable serenity and contentment, derived from an alignment between one's values and actions. Inner peace is frequently sought through practices that calm the mind and soothe the spirit, such as mindfulness, chanting, or silent reflection, which help dissolve everyday life's stresses and foster inner tranquility.

The rich tapestry of spirituality is not uniform but is characterised by a vibrant plurality. Across different cultures, the interpretation of what it means to be spiritual can vary significantly. In some cultures, spirituality is deeply entwined with ancestral veneration and the belief in a life-force that permeates all things, while in others, it might focus more on the individual's journey towards enlightenment or the dissolution of the self into a universal essence. This cultural variation enriches the global understanding of spirituality and provides various paths for individuals seeking spiritual depth.

Moreover, within any given culture, individual experiences of spirituality can vary widely. Two people from the same cultural background might adopt different spiritual paths—one might find deep spiritual connection in nature and solitude, while the other finds similar solace in community-oriented rituals or in the arts. This individual diversity underscores the deeply personal nature of spirituality, which does not lend itself to a one-size-fits-all approach.

The flexible nature of spirituality also allows it to evolve with societal changes and personal developments. As individuals grow and change, so too might their spiritual needs and practices. This dynamic quality of spirituality makes it a lifelong companion to many, capable of providing guidance, comfort, and purpose through various stages of life.

By exploring the breadth and depth of spirituality, we enrich our understanding and enhance our respect for the diverse ways in which people seek meaning and connection in their lives. Far from being a mere aspect of human experience, spirituality represents a fundamental dimension of human existence, offering insights and methodologies for living that are as varied as they are profound. By understanding and embracing this diversity, we pave the way for a more inclusive and compassionate world where spiritual well-being is integral to the overall quest for a fulfilled and meaningful life.

Exploring the Heart of Spiritual Experience

The profound journey into the essence of spiritual experiences reveals a landscape marked by deep emotions, transformative thoughts, and pivotal actions. This exploration delves into the core elements that underpin the spiritual journey—elements that resonate across diverse cultures and philosophies, illustrating the universal nature of our quest for deeper understanding. These core elements, including a sense of awe, connectedness, the pursuit of meaning, and the experience of transcendence, serve as the foundational threads that weave together human spirituality's vast and varied tapestry.

Awe: The Gateway to Reverence

Awe acts as a powerful catalyst in spiritual experiences, serving as the initial spark that ignites a deeper exploration of the mysteries of existence. Encounters with the vastness of nature, the complexity of the universe, or the beauty of art often trigger it. Such experiences provoke a profound sense of wonder and reverence, a realization that there is something far greater than the self. This sensation of awe is crucial as it diminishes the ego, allowing individuals to transcend their ordinary concerns and embrace a broader, more inclusive perspective. It nurtures the humility necessary to approach the spiritual with an open heart and mind, paving the way for deeper revelations and insights.

Connectedness: The Fabric of the Universe

At the core of many spiritual traditions is the principle of connectedness, a pervasive sense that all of life is interwoven into a single, dynamic tapestry. This interconnectedness is not merely ecological or social but fundamentally spiritual, suggesting an underlying unity that binds the cosmos. Whether expressed through the concept of Indra's Net in Hinduism, the interbeing taught by Thich Nhat Hanh, or the mystical union described by Sufi poets, this sense of connectedness reinforces our relationship with each other and the entire universe. It dissolves the illusion of separation, fostering an empathetic understanding that each action, thought, and emotion has a ripple effect throughout the spiritual and material world.

The Quest for Meaning and Purpose

Central to spiritual life is the quest for meaning and purpose, which compels individuals to look beyond the superficial layers of life to uncover the underlying reasons for existence. This quest is not confined to deciphering life's grand narrative but includes seeking significance in day-to-day experiences. It challenges individuals to live authentically according to their values and beliefs, transforming routine actions into expressions of deeper spiritual truths. Engaging in this quest provides direction and motivation and offers comfort in times of uncertainty and change, suggesting that each life has a unique role and purpose within the broader cosmic drama.

Transcendence: Beyond the Self

Transcendence involves stepping beyond the self or the ordinary experiences of reality, accessing a higher state of being that offers a new perspective on everything. This aspect of spirituality can be transformative, providing a glimpse of the divine, the infinite, or simply the interconnectedness of all things. Experiences of transcendence can occur through meditation, prayer, ritual, or sometimes spontaneously, granting insights that are often described as life-changing. They lift the veil between the mundane and the sacred, revealing the depth and richness of life that typically lies hidden beneath the everyday.

Integration: Manifesting Spirituality in Everyday Life

The true measure of these spiritual experiences lies in their integration into everyday life. It is not enough to encounter awe, feel connected, seek meaning, or experience transcendence; these elements must influence how one lives, interacts, and makes choices. This integration is perhaps the most challenging aspect of spirituality, as it requires constant attention and effort to apply spiritual insights to daily actions and decisions.

The journey through these core elements of spirituality is not linear but cyclical, with each aspect influencing and enhancing the others. Together, they form a robust framework for understanding the nature of spiritual experiences and their profound impact on personal and collective life. Through the continuous exploration of these elements, spirituality reveals itself not as a static set of beliefs or practices but as a dynamic, evolving path that profoundly shapes how we view the world and our place within it. This path, walked with intention and awareness, leads to personal fulfilment and a deeper appreciation of the complexity and beauty of life itself.

The Healing Power of Spiritual Practice

The interplay between spirituality and well-being is a subject of increasing interest, particularly in the realm of psychological and physical health. An exploration into the roles of spiritual practices such as meditation, prayer, and mindfulness reveals a significant positive impact on health outcomes, emotional resilience, and the overall quality of life. This profound connection underlines the potential of spirituality to serve not just as a personal solace but also as a practical tool for fostering well-being.

Spiritual Practices and Mental Health

The influence of spiritual practices on mental health is well-documented, with meditation and mindfulness at the forefront of contemporary wellness strategies. These practices, deeply rooted in spiritual traditions, contribute significantly to mental health by reducing symptoms of stress and anxiety. Meditation, for instance, enables individuals to achieve a state of deep peace and relaxation, which counteracts the arousal state triggered by stress and anxiety. Meditation enhances clarity and focus by promoting a calm mind, allowing for greater emotional regulation.

Mindfulness, a practice of being fully present and engaged in the moment without judgement, further extends these benefits by helping individuals cultivate a heightened awareness of their thoughts and feelings. This awareness is crucial for interrupting habitual reactions to stress, such as rumination and worry, and fosters a more reflective rather than reactive approach to challenges. Such practices decrease stress and enhance aspects of cognitive functioning, such as attention, concentration, and decision-making.

Physical Health and Spiritual Discipline

The impact of spiritual practices extends beyond mental health to influence physical well-being. Regular engagement in activities such as yoga and Tai Chi, combining physical movement with a spiritual or mindful focus, has improved physical health. These activities reduce blood pressure, alleviate chronic pain, and improve sleep quality, all of which are crucial components of overall health.

Moreover, spiritual disciplines often promote a holistic approach to health, advocating for balanced lifestyles that include proper nutrition, adequate exercise, and sufficient rest. These lifestyle choices, encouraged through spiritual teachings, contribute directly to better health outcomes. Furthermore, the peace and inner stability derived from spiritual practices can boost the immune system, making the body better equipped to handle illness and recover from disease.

Emotional Resilience through Spiritual Connection

Another significant aspect of spirituality's impact on well-being is its role in building emotional resilience. Spiritual practices foster a strong sense of meaning and purpose, which is essential in coping with life's adversities. The perspective gained through spiritual growth enables individuals to see beyond their immediate circumstances and appreciate a broader, more positive outlook on life. This perspective is incredibly resilient in the face of life's challenges, providing a buffer against despair and hopelessness.

Prayer, for instance, offers a profound source of comfort and strength in times of trouble, connecting individuals to a higher power and providing a sense of support and hope. This connection can be a critical resource in times of emotional turmoil, offering solace and a strong foundation of faith and hope that may lead to faster emotional recovery.

Enhancing Quality of Life

Ultimately, the integration of spiritual practices into daily life has a cumulative effect on improving the quality of life. These practices enhance one's ability to experience joy, peace, and fulfillment. They help individuals cultivate a sense of gratitude and appreciation for life's blessings, which are linked to higher levels of happiness and satisfaction.

Moreover, spirituality can enrich relationships, fostering deeper connections with others through shared values and compassionate understanding. This improvement in relational dynamics can lead to more supportive and fulfilling interpersonal interactions, which are crucial for emotional well-being.

A Holistic Approach to Health

Exploring spirituality's role in enhancing well-being illustrates that these practices are not merely escapist routines but effective methods for improving health and happiness. They provide tools for not only coping with life's difficulties but also enhancing life's quality through greater health, emotional stability, and deeper personal satisfaction. As the understanding of these connections deepens, spirituality is likely to play an increasingly prominent role in holistic health approaches, affirming its value not only for personal spiritual fulfillment but also as a vital component of overall health and well-being.

By embracing spirituality in its various forms, individuals open themselves to a world of profound health benefits, underscoring the essential nature of the spirit in cultivating a fulfilling and healthy life.

Chapter 2: Historical Overview of Spiritual Traditions

Human history is rich with spiritual exploration, a journey that spans every culture and epoch. As we delve into the historical tapestry of spiritual traditions in this chapter, we uncover how spirituality has shaped the identities, philosophies, and societies of human beings across the millennia. This exploration offers a panoramic view of the spiritual impulses that have driven human beings to seek meaning beyond the visible, tangible world.

From the primal rhythms of ancient shamanistic rituals to the intricate theologies of modern religions, spiritual practices have both responded to and reflected the environments in which they developed. The quest for understanding and connection with something greater than oneself appears to be a universal human experience, manifesting uniquely across different landscapes and epochs.

We begin with the ancient civilizations, where spirituality was often inseparably linked to daily survival and understanding the forces of nature. These early spiritual practices laid the foundational beliefs that would echo through time, influencing successive generations' views of the cosmos and their place within it. As civilizations grew, so too did their spiritual narratives, evolving into complex systems of gods and goddesses, rituals, and ethics that sought to order the universe and human behavior.

The chapter progresses through the development of the major world religions, which structured spiritual thought into systems that not only offered explanations for the mysteries of life but also provided moral frameworks and communal identities. With their prophets, sacred texts, and dogmas, these religions spread across continents, shaping politics, culture, and individual lives profoundly.

We also explore the rich spiritual traditions of indigenous peoples, whose often overlooked practices emphasize a deep connection with the environment and community. These traditions remind us of the diverse expressions of spirituality and the various ways human beings relate to the mystical aspects of existence.

In examining the interplay between different spiritual traditions, we see periods of synthesis and conflict, as ideas were exchanged or resisted, leading to the evolution of spiritual practices that were both inclusive and exclusive. The influence of the Enlightenment introduced new challenges to spiritual authority, prompting a shift towards personal spirituality that has characterized much of modern spiritual thought.

This historical overview contextualizes the myriad ways in which humanity has engaged with the spiritual and sets the stage for understanding current spiritual dynamics and the continuing evolution of spiritual practices. As we trace this journey, we gain insight into the enduring quest for transcendence, meaning, and connection that continues to resonate across the globe, shaping and being shaped by the ever-changing human condition.

Origins of Spirituality in Ancient Civilizations

The origins of spirituality in ancient civilizations provide a fascinating glimpse into the early human quest to understand the cosmos and their place within it. The spiritual practices of Mesopotamia, Egypt, the Indus Valley, and ancient China reflect the ingenuity of early societies and highlight how these initial beliefs and rituals were deeply intertwined with aspects of daily life, governance, and cosmic understanding. Exploring these ancient systems offers invaluable insights into the foundational structures from which later spiritual traditions evolved.

Mesopotamia: Cradle of Divine Kingship

In ancient Mesopotamia, the world's earliest known civilization, spirituality was a complex blend of mythology, religion, and kingship. The Mesopotamians believed in a pantheon of gods who actively influenced every aspect of human life and the natural world. This belief system was intricately linked to their understanding of agriculture, astronomy, and law. The ziggurats, towering temple complexes, were not just places of worship but also served as administrative centres where divine and royal mandates were intertwined. Rulers were often seen as divine or semi-divine mediators between the gods and the people, tasked with maintaining the gods' favour to ensure the prosperity and stability of their city-states.

Egypt: Harmony and Eternity

The ancient Egyptians' spiritual practices were centred around the concepts of order, harmony, and eternity. They believed in a cosmological order called Ma'at, which represented truth, balance, and justice, and was essential for maintaining the harmony of the universe. The pharaohs, considered gods on earth, were seen as guardians of this cosmic order. Spirituality was embedded in their monumental architecture, such as pyramids and tombs, designed to ensure life's continuity after death. The elaborate rituals performed in these spaces aimed to secure divine protection and immortality, reflecting the Egyptians' deep concern with eternal life and their profound connection to the divine.

The Indus Valley: Rituals of Purity and Prosperity

The spirituality of the Indus Valley civilization, contemporary with those of Egypt and Mesopotamia, remains somewhat enigmatic due to the undeciphered script of this culture. However, archaeological findings, such as the great baths and numerous figurines, suggest that rituals of purity and fertility played significant roles. These practices likely served to align the society with the natural and supernatural forces to ensure health, agricultural success, and overall societal prosperity. With their sophisticated water management systems, the urban planning of cities like Mohenjo-Daro indicates a highly organized society where spiritual and practical life were seamlessly integrated.

Ancient China: The Mandate of Heaven

In ancient China, spirituality was closely linked with the philosophy of the cosmos and the governance mandate. The Mandate of Heaven was a central idea; it held that the legitimacy of rulers was granted by a celestial order, reflecting the moral force of the universe. This mandate was not permanent but could be lost through tyranny or incompetence, indicating that the rulers had to maintain high moral standards and rule justly to retain divine favour. Chinese spirituality was deeply philosophical, embodied in the teachings of Confucianism and Daoism, which emphasized moral integrity, harmony with nature, and the importance of ritual in daily life.

Foundational Impact on Later Traditions

The spiritual practices of these ancient civilizations laid the groundwork for the complex tapestry of later spiritual and religious developments. They established the fundamental human inclination early on to link the celestial and the terrestrial, to seek harmony between human existence and the larger forces of the universe. Each culture's unique approach to spirituality offers a mirror into their worldview and the values they held sacred, from the divine rulership of Mesopotamia and Egypt to the moral and philosophical richness of the Indus Valley and ancient China.

Understanding these ancient spiritual practices enriches our comprehension of human history and spirituality's role in shaping our earliest civilizations. It allows us to appreciate the profound ways in which our ancestors sought to understand and influence the world around them through spiritual means, setting the stage for the diverse array of spiritual paths that would follow throughout human history.

Development of Spiritual Traditions in Classical Antiquity

The classical age, particularly in Greece and Rome, marked a significant period in the development of spiritual traditions that profoundly impacted Western thought and beyond. This era was characterized by remarkable intellectual exploration and religious syncretism, where philosophical inquiry and the integration of diverse religious practices shaped a complex spiritual landscape. The contributions of seminal philosophers such as Socrates, Plato, and Aristotle in Greece, alongside the religious syncretism observed in the Roman Empire, offer a rich tapestry of spiritual evolution that resonates through the ages.

The Philosophical Foundations of Greece

In Greece, the spiritual landscape was intricately tied to the philosophical pursuits of its most distinguished thinkers. Socrates, Plato, and Aristotle each contributed uniquely to the spiritual and philosophical discourse, exploring the nature of truth, ethics, and the existence of the soul, which would lay the groundwork for both Eastern and Western spiritual traditions.

With his dialectical method, Socrates challenged the Athenians to question their understanding of virtues and the essence of a good life. His approach was philosophical and deeply spiritual, as he sought to align the soul towards greater truth and virtue through rigorous self-examination and dialogue. Socrates famously believed that an unexamined life was not worth living, a statement underlining his commitment to spiritual and moral inquiry.

Plato, Socrates' most famous pupil, expanded on his teacher's ideas and introduced the theory of Forms, positing a transcendent realm of perfect and immutable forms representing the truest essence of things in the material world. For Plato, understanding these forms was crucial for achieving spiritual insight and moral virtue. His work in the "Republic" and "Timaeus," among others, not only questioned the nature of reality but also offered a vision of the soul's ascent to spiritual enlightenment, influenced by Pythagorean and Orphic religious thought.

Aristotle took a somewhat different approach by grounding his philosophy more in the observable world. He developed a comprehensive system of thought that included metaphysics, ethics, and politics, where he emphasized the purpose and function (telos) of beings and objects. For Aristotle, the pursuit of one's purpose or the highest good—eudaimonia—was essential for achieving a well-lived life. His notion of the 'Golden Mean', where virtue is balanced between excess and deficiency, guided ethical conduct and outlined a path towards achieving spiritual balance and well-being.

Roman Religious Syncretism

The Roman Empire, with its vast territories and amalgamation of cultures, showcased an unparalleled religious syncretism that absorbed and adapted the deities and rituals of conquered peoples. This integration reflected Rome's pragmatic approach to governance and spirituality, where incorporating diverse religious practices was both a means of cultural assimilation and a method to maintain political harmony.

The Romans adopted Greek gods and merged them with their own, leading to a pantheon where Zeus became Jupiter, and Hera became Juno, among others. This syncretism extended beyond Greek influences to include Egyptian, Celtic, and Eastern deities, each bringing their own spiritual practices and rituals into the Roman fold.

The cults of Isis from Egypt and Mithras from Persia, in particular, gained substantial followings and influenced Roman spiritual life with their mysteries and rites, which offered personal salvation and mystical union with the divine.

The religious landscape in Rome was also marked by the state religion, which was closely linked with the power and authority of the emperor. The imperial cult, which deified past emperors and sometimes even the reigning emperor, was a distinct spiritual practice that blurred the lines between political loyalty and religious devotion. This phenomenon highlighted the unique role of spirituality in Roman public and political life.

Legacy and Influence

Classical antiquity's philosophical and religious fabric left a lasting legacy on spiritual thought. Greek philosophy's rational and ethical inquiries provided foundational texts for later Christian and Islamic theologians, who found in them a source of wisdom and intellectual support for their own spiritual doctrines. Meanwhile, the Roman practice of religious syncretism demonstrated the potential for diverse spiritual practices to coexist and evolve within a broad imperial context.

The spiritual traditions of Greece and Rome thus not only influenced each other but also set the stage for the development of spiritual thought in later periods. They taught us the value of philosophical rigor and the importance of integrating diverse perspectives, shaping a legacy that continues to influence contemporary spiritual practices and philosophical inquiries. Through their achievements, classical antiquity remains a pivotal period in spiritual evolution, demonstrating the enduring human quest to understand the divine and our place within the cosmos.

Spiritual Convergences and Divergences in the Axial Age

The period known as the Axial Age, approximately 800 to 200 BCE, stands as a crucible moment in the annals of spiritual history. This era witnessed an unprecedented flourish of philosophical and religious thought across various regions of the world, laying down the foundational beliefs that continue to shape spiritual discourse today. Remarkably, these developments occurred largely in isolation from each other across China, India, and the Middle East, yet they shared strikingly similar thematic concerns—questions about the nature of the divine, the self, and the path to spiritual fulfillment.

Emergence of Transformative Spiritual Ideas

In China, this period marked the genesis of Confucianism and Taoism, two philosophical traditions with deep spiritual undertones that offered contrasting paths to societal harmony and personal virtue. Confucius set forth a system focused on ethics, familial respect, and social duty, positing that a well-ordered society depended on the righteous behavior of its individuals, beginning from the family unit and extending to the state. In contrast, Laozi, the legendary founder of Taoism, proposed a return to a life of simplicity and spontaneity governed by the Tao, or the 'Way', a fundamental and transcendent order that flows through all existence, often in inexplicable ways.

Meanwhile, in India, the Upanishads, a series of philosophical texts, elaborated on the earlier Vedic traditions and introduced key concepts of Hinduism such as Brahman (the universal spirit) and Atman (the individual soul), emphasizing their ultimate unity. This period also saw the birth of Buddhism, founded by Siddhartha Gautama, the Buddha, who preached the Middle Way as a path to enlightenment—eschewing both severe asceticism and worldly indulgence to achieve Nirvana, a state of liberation from suffering and desire.

In the Middle East, monotheism became more pronounced with the Hebrew prophets, who articulated a vision of an omnipotent, singular God who was not only the creator of the universe but also actively involved in its governance through a covenantal relationship with his people. This theological stance marked a significant divergence from the polytheistic and often locality-bound deities prevalent in neighboring cultures.

Convergences and Divergences in Spiritual Perspectives

Despite the geographical and cultural distances that separated these regions, the Axial Age spiritual leaders converged on several core principles. They largely moved away from the capricious polytheism that had dominated earlier epochs to embrace more abstract, profound conceptions of the divine and its relationship with humanity. Moreover, they shared a concern with the condition of the human soul, emphasizing ethical living and inner spiritual development as the means to higher existential states.

However, their approaches to these questions exhibited notable divergences reflective of their distinct cultural and historical contexts. For instance, while Confucianism stressed ethical conduct and duty to the community as pathways to spiritual harmony, Buddhism focused on personal suffering and the pursuit of individual enlightenment. Similarly, the monotheistic focus of Hebrew prophets promoted a unique and unbreakable bond between God and humanity, which contrasted with the more impersonal Brahman-Atman relationship proposed in Hinduism.

Pathways to Spiritual Fulfillment

These traditions' pathways to spiritual fulfillment also reflect their foundational differences. The Middle Eastern monotheistic trajectory was intrinsically linked with obedience to divine law and moral rectitude as dictated by scriptural texts. In contrast, Hinduism and Buddhism offered a more introspective route, emphasizing meditation, renunciation of earthly attachments, and the rigorous pursuit of spiritual knowledge to dissolve the ego and realize the self's deeper or divine nature.

Taoism, with its principles of non-action (wu wei) and naturalness, advocated for a life in harmony with the natural world, viewing true wisdom and peace as arising from a life lived in accordance with the Tao, beyond conventional moralities and societal structures.

Legacy of the Axial Age

The spiritual philosophies and religious practices that crystallized during the Axial Age continue to influence billions of lives across the globe. Their enduring legacy is not just in the religious institutions they spawned but in the fundamental shift they marked from external ritualistic worship to internal moral and spiritual introspection. This age was a pivotal chapter in human history that shaped the spiritual landscapes of entire civilizations and introduced new dimensions to our understanding of the divine, the universe, and ourselves.

The cross-cultural echo of similar spiritual questions and answers from this period suggests a shared human propensity to seek connection with something greater than oneself, whether manifested through divine laws, ethical living, or meditative insight. This Axial Age, therefore, not only highlights the diversity of spiritual expression but also underscores the unity underlying humanity's quest for meaning and fulfillment.

The Spread and Evolution of Abrahamic Religions

The Abrahamic religions—Judaism, Christianity, and Islam—comprise billions of adherents' spiritual and cultural heritage worldwide. These faiths, interconnected by their monotheistic foundation and historical narratives rooted in the figure of Abraham, have not only shaped personal beliefs and communal laws but have also profoundly influenced global history, culture, and politics. This article traces the origins, expansion, and evolution of these three major religious traditions, exploring their foundational texts, key figures, and the historical milestones that led to their widespread adoption and adaptation across diverse cultures and continents.

Origins and Foundational Texts

Judaism, the oldest of the three, began in the lands of ancient Canaan, with its theological foundations and historical narratives embedded in the Hebrew Bible, particularly the Torah. Central to Jewish belief is the covenant relationship between the God of Israel and Abraham, and subsequently with Isaac, Jacob, and Moses, who is regarded as the lawgiver. The covenant, with its divine laws received on Mount Sinai, not only outlined a religious structure but also set forth ethical and moral principles guiding personal and communal life.

Christianity emerged in the first century AD, rooted in the life and teachings of Jesus of Nazareth, whom Christians regard as the prophesied Messiah and Son of God. The New Testament, which includes the Gospels, Acts, Epistles, and Revelation, records the life of Jesus, his teachings, crucifixion, and resurrection, and the early days of the Christian community. Christianity distinguished itself from Judaism through the concept of Jesus as the Messiah and the universal nature of his message, inviting Jews and all humanity to join in a new covenant with God.

Islam, founded in the 7th century AD by the Prophet Muhammad in Mecca, is based on the Quran, believed by Muslims to be the final revelation by God (Allah), a continuation and completion of the truths found in Jewish and Christian texts. The Hadith, records of sayings and actions of Muhammad, complements the Quran and guides Muslims in practice. Islam's key elements include the Five Pillars, which prescribe monotheism, prayer, fasting, charity, and pilgrimage, and its law, Sharia, which has governed religious practice and daily life.

Expansion and Historical Milestones

The expansion of these religions over centuries is a saga of spiritual appeal, conquest, conversion, and sometimes conflict. Judaism spread initially through the tribes of Israel and later through diasporas caused by conquests and exiles, such as the Babylonian Captivity and the Roman destruction of Jerusalem. Despite its smaller numbers relative to Christianity and Islam, Judaism's influence on subsequent Abrahamic religions and its resilience in maintaining a distinct religious and cultural identity have been profound.

Christianity's growth was catalyzed by several factors, including its embrace by the Roman Empire under Emperor Constantine in the 4th century. This legitimised Christianity and facilitated its spread across Europe and later to other continents through colonialism, mission work, and migration. The schism between the Roman Catholic Church and the Eastern Orthodox Church, and later the Protestant Reformation, were significant events that not only altered the religious landscape of Christianity but also influenced European political histories and philosophical thought.

Islam expanded rapidly after the death of Muhammad through conquests and peaceful conversions. By the end of the 8th century, Islamic empires stretched from the Iberian Peninsula to the borders of China. Key milestones include the Sunni-Shia split following the death of the Prophet Muhammad, the establishment of the various Caliphates, and the spread of Islam to Sub-Saharan Africa, Central Asia, and Southeast Asia through trade and Sufi missionaries.

Adaptation Across Cultures

As these religions spread, they adapted to and were shaped by local cultures and societies, leading to a rich diversity within each faith. Judaism's adaptations are seen in the varying rites and customs among Ashkenazi, Sephardi, and Mizrahi Jews. Christianity, with its myriad denominations, incorporates local traditions and languages into its worship and practice worldwide. Similarly, Islam is practised differently worldwide, with cultural variations seen in practices from the Middle East, South Asia, Southeast Asia, and Africa.

The journey of the Abrahamic religions is a testament to their enduring appeal and adaptability. From their ancient origins to their contemporary manifestations, these faiths have not only survived but thrived, continually influencing and being influenced by the myriad cultures with which they interact. Their histories are not only spiritual narratives but also chronicles of human civilization, reflecting the complex interplay between faith and the diverse identities of its adherents. Through this historical lens, we gain not only a deeper understanding of each faith's unique path but also a broader view of how spiritual traditions shape and are shaped by the ever-evolving human landscape.

Indigenous and Pagan Spiritual Systems

The spiritual systems of indigenous and pagan communities around the globe showcase a rich tapestry of beliefs, rituals, and connections to the natural world that differ significantly from the doctrinal religions more commonly discussed in the global North. From the expansive plains of North America to the dense forests of Sub-Saharan Africa and the rugged landscapes of Australia, indigenous spiritualities offer a profound insight into the symbiotic relationship between humans and nature, a reverence for ancestors, and the pivotal role of rituals in daily life. These traditions, often passed down orally through generations, continue to survive and influence modern spiritual practices, reflecting a resilience and adaptability that enriches our understanding of spirituality itself.

Native American Spirituality

In North America, the spiritual practices of Native American tribes exemplify a deep connection to the land and its spirits. These beliefs are not uniform but vary widely among tribes, each possessing its own rituals, myths, and spiritual practices intrinsically linked to the tribe's specific geographic locale. Common elements include animism—the belief that natural objects and phenomena possess a spiritual essence. Rituals such as the Sun Dance, potlatch ceremonies, and vision quests serve as rites of passage and as ways to maintain harmony with the spiritual forces that govern the world. The use of totems, or spirit beings symbolizing animals or ancestors, underscores the profound ancestral reverence and the spiritual guardianship they are believed to provide.

Sub-Saharan African Religions

In Sub-Saharan Africa, the spiritual systems are equally diverse and vibrant, encompassing a vast array of ethnic groups each with their own spiritual traditions. These religions typically emphasize ancestor worship, believing that the deceased play an active role in the affairs of the living. This connection is maintained through libations, rituals, and the invocation of ancestors during important community decisions. Animism and pantheism are prevalent, with a strong belief in spirits residing in natural elements such as rivers, mountains, and trees, often worshipped as gods or ancestors' manifestations. Rituals and ceremonies in these communities are not merely spiritual practices but are integral to maintaining the people's social fabric and cultural identity.

Australian Aboriginal Spirituality

The spirituality of Australian Aboriginal peoples is one of the oldest continuous religious traditions in the world, deeply rooted in the concept of the Dreamtime. This foundational mythology explains the origins and structure of the universe and the creation stories of life on Earth. Dreamtime is not considered a myth or a past event but a continuous, living reality that is accessible through rituals, storytelling, and rock art. Land is not just a physical place but a living entity filled with spiritual significance, encompassing ancestral beings whose presence is still felt and revered. Sacred sites, often natural landmarks, play a crucial role in these spiritual and cultural practices, serving as focal points for ceremonies that ensure the continuity of the natural and spiritual order.

Influence on Modern Spiritual Practices

Despite the pressures of modernization and the often devastating impacts of colonization, many of these indigenous spiritual practices have not only survived but have seen a resurgence in recent years as part of broader cultural revival movements. They have also significantly influenced contemporary spiritual practices around the world. The concepts of environmental stewardship, holistic health, and community-oriented living, central to many indigenous religions, have been embraced by modern movements seeking sustainable and balanced ways of living. Practices such as meditation, using natural medicines, and celebrating the solstices are examples of indigenous influences permeating broader cultural practices.

The respect for nature, deep communal bonds, and ritualistic healing found in these spiritual systems counterbalance modern Western societies' often individualistic and materialistic orientations. They remind us of the diverse ways humans can connect with the spiritual dimensions of their lives and offer valuable lessons on the importance of community, respect for nature, and the spiritual value of tradition and ritual.

As we continue to explore and integrate these ancient wisdoms into contemporary life, it becomes clear that the spiritual systems of indigenous and pagan peoples are not relics of the past but vital, living traditions that continue to offer profound insights into the nature of existence, the universe, and the interconnectivity of all life. Their continued relevance and resilience highlight the universal human quest for meaning and connection in an ever-changing world.

Part II: Diverse Spiritual Paths

Chapter 3: Eastern Traditions

The spiritual landscape of the East offers a rich tapestry of philosophies, religious practices, and ethical teachings that have not only shaped the lives of billions in Asia but have also profoundly impacted the global understanding of spirituality. This chapter delves into the profound and diverse traditions of Eastern spirituality, exploring how these ancient practices have nurtured a deep connection between humans and the cosmos, influenced societies, and offered pathways to personal enlightenment and communal harmony.

From the verdant riverbanks of the Indian subcontinent to the mist-shrouded mountains of China and the serene temples of Japan, Eastern spiritual traditions such as Hinduism, Buddhism, Taoism, Confucianism, and Shinto have developed over millennia. These traditions each present a unique view of existence, morality, and the ultimate goal of life, whether it is liberation from the cycle of rebirth, harmony with the universal Tao, or living a life of righteousness according to ethical principles.

In this chapter, we will begin by exploring the intricate world of Hinduism with its vast pantheon of gods and profound philosophical texts that guide adherents toward spiritual liberation. We will then trace the path of Buddhism from its inception under the Bodhi tree in India to its spread across Asia, transforming into a multitude of schools and sects that interpret the teachings of the Buddha to seek enlightenment.

Following personal liberation and enlightenment, we will examine Taoism and Confucianism, two pillars of Chinese thought that illustrate the dual approach to living in harmony with the natural world and society. While Taoism teaches the way of effortless action and harmony with the Tao, Confucianism emphasizes moral rectitude and social order through dutiful action.

Further, we will look at Shinto, Japan's indigenous spirituality, which celebrates the sacredness of nature and kami (spiritual presences), reflecting the deep animistic roots of Japanese culture. Additionally, we will touch on the less widespread but equally rich traditions of

Jainism and Sikhism, which have contributed significantly to the spiritual and ethical fabric of Indian society.

Each of these traditions offers a set of beliefs and a way of life that has sustained communities, fostered peace, and inspired philosophical and artistic achievements throughout history. As we explore these traditions, we will consider how they compare with each other, their interactions over centuries, and their adaptations in the modern world.

This journey through Eastern spiritual traditions will reveal the depth and diversity of spiritual thought and practice in Asia, highlighting how these ancient wisdoms continue to offer insight and guidance in a rapidly changing world. As we explore these paths, we uncover the distinctive characteristics of each tradition and the shared human quest for meaning and connection that transcends geographic and cultural boundaries.

Hinduism: Diversity and Devotion

One of the world's oldest living religions, Hinduism presents a complex and vibrant spiritual landscape marked by a profound diversity of beliefs, practices, and philosophical schools. Emerging in the Indian subcontinent, Hinduism has developed over thousands of years, offering a unique blend of myth, philosophy, and ritual that continues to adapt and flourish in contemporary societies. This article explores the origins and evolution of Hinduism, delving into its key concepts, myriad deities, and its central philosophical tenets of dharma, karma, and moksha.

Historical Roots and Evolution

Hinduism's roots can be traced back to the ancient Indus Valley civilization around 2000 BCE and later to the Vedic period resulting from the Indo-Aryan migration. These early stages laid down the ritualistic and philosophical foundations of what would evolve into Hinduism through the sacred texts known as the Vedas. Over centuries, this religious practice saw significant transformations, incorporating various cultural and spiritual elements from around the region, contributing to the rich tapestry of beliefs and practices known today as Hinduism.

Deities and Rituals

At the heart of Hinduism lies a vast pantheon of gods and goddesses, each embodying different aspects of life and the cosmos. Major deities such as Brahma, Vishnu, and Shiva play central roles in the universe's creation, preservation, and destruction. However, Hinduism also features an extensive array of other deities, each associated with specific aspects of life and moral values, which are worshipped in a myriad of rituals. These rituals, ranging from simple daily prayers at household shrines to elaborate ceremonies at grand temples, serve as vital connections between the divine and the devotee, facilitating a direct and personal interaction with the divine.

Philosophical Schools and Key Concepts

Its intellectual depth and philosophical diversity distinguishes Hinduism. The religion is underpinned by several core concepts that guide its adherents' moral and spiritual life. Dharma, or duty, is a central principle that refers to the righteousness and moral values dictated by one's position in life and the universe. Karma, the law of cause and effect, postulates that every action produces corresponding positive or negative reactions, influencing future lives through reincarnation.

Another critical concept is moksha, or liberation from the cycle of birth and rebirth (samsara), which is the ultimate spiritual goal for many Hindus. Achieving moksha involves realizing one's true spiritual nature and transcending earthly desires and attachments.

Devotional Paths

The path of bhakti or devotional worship, is one of the principal and most cherished routes to spiritual fulfillment in Hinduism. It emphasizes loving devotion towards a personal god, such as Vishnu or Shiva or their avatars like Krishna and Rama. This devotion is expressed through singing hymns, chanting mantras, and participating in rituals and festivals, which not only serve to express and nurture love for the divine but also foster community bonds among followers.

Sacred Texts and Epic Narratives

Hinduism's philosophical foundation is enriched by a vast corpus of sacred texts, from the ancient Vedas to the philosophical treatises of the Upanishads and the Ramayana and Mahabharata epic narratives. Each text serves multiple purposes—documenting the religious rites, philosophies, and the moral and ethical guidelines that help guide the conduct of individuals and communities.

The Bhagavad Gita, part of the Mahabharata, holds a special place in Hindu literature and philosophy. It addresses the moral and philosophical dilemmas faced by the prince Arjuna, whom Krishna, an avatar of Vishnu, guides. The Gita discusses various paths to spiritual realization, making it a crucial spiritual guide for seekers within and beyond Hinduism.

Hinduism's remarkable adaptability and tolerance for diverse practices and philosophies have allowed it to endure and thrive for thousands of years. Its deep roots in ritual and a sophisticated array of philosophical teachings accommodate a wide range of spiritual expressions and pursuits. From the high philosophical discourses about the nature of reality and the universe to the heartfelt devotions of its followers, Hinduism continues to be a source of guidance, inspiration, and spiritual nourishment for millions of adherents around the world. Through its rich mosaic of deities, rituals, and sacred texts, Hinduism connects individuals to their ancient past and meets their contemporary spiritual needs in an ever-evolving world.

Buddhism: The Path of Enlightenment

Buddhism, originating in the foothills of the Himalayas, has unfolded over the centuries as a profound spiritual journey toward enlightenment, influencing millions across Asia and, more recently, the world. Founded on the teachings of Siddhartha Gautama, known as the Buddha, Buddhism extends an invitation to explore the nature of suffering and the pathways to its cessation through deep understanding and ethical living.

The Life of Siddhartha Gautama

Siddhartha Gautama's journey to becoming the Buddha begins with his birth into a royal family in what is now Nepal, around the 5th century BCE. His life as a prince was one of luxury, and he was shielded from human suffering. However, encounters with the harsh realities of life — old age, sickness, and death — spurred a profound spiritual crisis and a quest for deeper meaning. Siddhartha renounced his royal heritage, adopting the life of an ascetic in search of truth.

After years of rigorous ascetic practices, he realized that neither extreme indulgence nor extreme deprivation led to true understanding. This insight led him to the path of moderation, or the Middle Way, culminating in his enlightenment under the Bodhi tree. He emerged with profound insights into the nature of existence, which would form the core of his teachings.

Core Teachings: The Four Noble Truths and the Eightfold Path

The essence of the Buddha's enlightenment was encapsulated in the Four Noble Truths. The first truth, Dukkha, asserts that life is permeated with suffering which is inherent in the transient nature of the world. The second truth, Samudaya, identifies desire and attachment as the causes of this suffering. The third truth, Nirodha, presents the possibility of cessation of suffering through the relinquishment of these desires. The fourth and final truth, Magga, prescribes the Eightfold Path as the means to overcome these attachments and attain Nirvana, a state of liberation and freedom from suffering.

The Eightfold Path offers a comprehensive guideline for ethical and mental development, focusing on right understanding, right intent, right speech, right action, right livelihood, right effort, right mindfulness, and right concentration. These practices are not sequential but interdependent and encompass ethical conduct, mental discipline, and wisdom.

Major Branches of Buddhism

Buddhism's spread across Asia led to the evolution of various schools and practices, primarily categorized into Theravada, Mahayana, and Vajrayana traditions. Theravada, or the "Teaching of the Elders," focuses on the monastic community and the meditation practices aimed at achieving personal enlightenment. It remains prevalent in Sri Lanka, Thailand, Burma, Laos, and Cambodia.

Mahayana, or the "Great Vehicle," emerged later and introduced the ideal of the Bodhisattva, a being who seeks Buddha-nature for the benefit of all sentient beings. This form of Buddhism emphasizes compassion and is influential in China, Korea, Japan, and Vietnam.

Vajrayana, or the "Diamond Vehicle," incorporates elements of both Theravada and Mahayana, along with esoteric practices and rituals that are believed to accelerate the path to enlightenment. It is primarily practiced in Tibet, Bhutan, and Mongolia and is known for its rich ritualistic traditions and the profound use of meditation techniques.

Mindfulness and Meditation

Central to Buddhist practice across all traditions is the emphasis on mindfulness and meditation. Mindfulness involves a keen awareness of the present moment, a direct and non-judgmental observation of one's thoughts, feelings, and sensations. Meditation, particularly insight meditation (Vipassana) and concentration meditation (Samatha), are crucial practices that foster deep mental focus and the development of insight into the nature of reality.

The Pursuit of Nirvana

Buddhism's ultimate goal is to attain Nirvana, a state beyond all suffering and the endless cycle of birth and rebirth (samsara). Nirvana is reached through the cultivation of wisdom, ethical conduct, and mental discipline, leading to the realization of the true nature of existence.

Buddhism's teachings on suffering, impermanence, and the interdependent nature of reality offer a profound wisdom that has resonated with diverse cultures over millennia. Through its rich philosophical insights and practical emphasis on meditation and ethics, Buddhism continues to offer paths to spiritual liberation and enlightenment, inviting followers from across the globe to embark on a journey of profound transformation and inner peace. This exploration into the essence of Buddhism reveals not just a religion, but a way of life that seeks to bring about a deeper understanding of the self and the world.

Taoism: The Way and Its Virtue

Taoism, an ancient Chinese philosophical and spiritual tradition, has woven its teachings into the fabric of Chinese culture, influencing art, politics, and medicine over millennia. Rooted in the enigmatic texts of the *Tao Te Ching* by Laozi and the profound writings of Zhuangzi, Taoism offers a unique perspective on the nature of existence and the path to harmony with the universe.

Foundational Texts of Taoism

The *Tao Te Ching*, attributed to the sage Laozi who is thought to have lived in the 6th century BCE, serves as the cornerstone of Taoist philosophy. Comprising 81 short chapters, this foundational text presents a series of poetic and often cryptic verses that contemplate the nature of the Tao (the Way) and how to live in accordance with it. The *Tao Te Ching* emphasizes themes of simplicity, humility, and the paradoxical nature of the universe, advocating for a life that flows naturally with the Tao's inherent order.

Zhuangzi, another seminal Taoist figure, expanded on these ideas in his eponymous text, which blends humor, allegory, and paradox to explore the limits of language and the importance of spontaneity. His work delves deeper into the Taoist attitude toward life, celebrating the freedom that comes from realizing the smallness of human concerns in the vastness of the universe.

Key Principles of Taoism

One of the central principles of Taoism is *Wu Wei*, often translated as "non-action" or "effortless action." This concept does not advocate passivity but suggests an approach to life where actions are aligned with the natural rhythms of the cosmos, executed without unnecessary force or resistance. *Wu Wei* is about finding the most effective way to achieve goals with minimal effort, emphasizing spontaneity and fluidity in all actions.

The principle of *Yin and Yang* symbolizes the world's dual nature, representing opposite but interconnected forces or energies. Yin (the receptive, feminine, dark, and passive principle) and Yang (the active, masculine, bright, and aggressive principle) are seen as fundamental elements of the universe that must balance each other to maintain harmony in the natural world and human life.

Harmony with the Tao

The ultimate goal in Taoism is to achieve harmony with the Tao, considered the essential, unnameable process of the universe. Adherents believe that by understanding the Tao, one can live a life of balance and peace. This harmony is pursued through practices such as Tai Chi, Qi Gong, and meditation, which help cultivate energy flow and mental focus, aligning the practitioner with the Tao's subtle presence in all things.

Influence on Chinese Culture

Taoism has profoundly influenced Chinese culture, particularly in the realms of art, politics, and medicine. In art, Taoist principles have fostered a deep appreciation for the beauty of the natural world, influencing landscape painting and calligraphy with an emphasis on simplicity, spontaneity, and the dynamic interplay of *Yin* and *Yang*. These artworks are not just representations but meditations on the essence of nature and the human place within it.

In politics, Taoist philosophy has at times provided a counterpoint to the rigid hierarchies and legalism prevalent in Chinese imperial governance. Its principles have encouraged leaders to rule with a light touch and consider their subjects' welfare by minimizing their interference in people's lives.

Taoist ideas have also been integral to traditional Chinese medicine, which views the human body as a microcosm of the universe that must maintain internal harmony to stay healthy. Practices such as acupuncture, herbal medicine, and dietary therapy seek to balance the body's vital energy, or *Qi*, consistent with Taoist thought.

Taoism offers a way to understand and interact with the world through a lens of balance, moderation, and alignment with the natural order. Its teachings encourage a deep connection to the rhythms of life, promoting peace, understanding, and health in personal and communal spheres. As we navigate the complexities of modern existence, the ancient wisdom of Taoism remains a guiding light for those seeking a harmonious and balanced approach to life's challenges. Through its profound philosophical insights and practical applications, Taoism continues offering timeless wisdom on living well.

Confucianism: Ethics and Order

Confucianism, rooted in the teachings of Confucius, has shaped the moral fabric and political structure of East Asian societies for centuries. This philosophy, more a way of life than a religious belief, emphasizes morality, social relationships, and justice, impacting everything from family dynamics to governmental policies. The enduring wisdom of Confucius, primarily recorded in the *Analects*, continues to offer profound insights into creating and maintaining social harmony and ethical governance.

Core Teachings of Confucius

The *Analects* of Confucius compile dialogues and sayings attributed to the sage and his disciples, outlining a philosophy focused on practical morality and ethics. Confucius posited that societal harmony could be achieved through the cultivation of individual virtue, which begins with sincere self-improvement and extends outward to influence family, community, and the state.

Key to Confucian ethics are the concepts of *ren* (benevolence or humaneness), *yi* (righteousness), and *li* (proper behavior or ritual propriety). *Ren* involves a compassionate attitude towards others, which Confucius considered essential to being fully human. *Yi* refers to the ability to do the right thing, while *li* encompasses the rituals and norms governing interactions within society, ensuring that respect and politeness underscore all human relationships.

Family Loyalty and Social Harmony

Confucianism places significant emphasis on family as the cornerstone of a stable society. Filial piety, or respect for one's parents and ancestors, is fundamental, extending to elder respect and loyalty in broader social contexts. This familial reverence ensures that each member of society understands their role and duties, which in theory leads to greater societal stability and harmony.

Confucius also stressed the importance of *Junzi* or "noble person." The *Junzi* practices self-discipline, demonstrates moral integrity, and works for the welfare of the community. Such leaders are expected to serve as moral exemplars who inspire ethical behavior in others.

Impact on Social and Political Philosophies

The influence of Confucian thought on the political systems of East Asia is profound and enduring. In imperial China, Korea, Japan, and Vietnam, Confucianism was adopted as the state philosophy, shaping political theories and practices. Confucian ideals were used to train civil servants and define legal systems, emphasizing meritocracy, loyalty, and duty to the ruler and state.

In modern times, while the political landscape has evolved, the ethical underpinnings of Confucianism still play a critical role in shaping cultural norms and government policies within East Asian societies. The emphasis on group harmony over individual rights, respect for authority, and the value of education continue to influence these societies deeply.

Rites, Rituals, and Education

Rituals in Confucianism are not merely religious ceremonies but are seen as essential to fostering respect and learning proper conduct. Through participation in rituals, individuals learn to put societal needs above personal desires, thereby maintaining social harmony. These rituals extend from significant public ceremonies to daily acts of respect and politeness.

Education is another pillar of Confucian thought, believed to be crucial for moral development and societal well-being. Confucius championed education as a means to cultivate wise and virtuous citizens, not limited to the elite but accessible to all, as a way to uplift society. The historical civil service examinations in China, heavily influenced by Confucianism, underscored this belief by linking government service to scholarly merit.

Confucianism, with its focus on ethical living, social responsibility, and educational attainment, provides a blueprint for personal development and societal stability. Its rich East Asian legacy testifies to the power of moral education and ethical governance in creating cohesive societies. Through the teachings of the *Analects*, Confucius' vision for a harmonious society, guided by wise and virtuous individuals, continues to resonate, offering timeless principles for ethical conduct and social integrity in the modern world.

Shinto: Kami and the Sacredness of Nature

Shinto, or 'the way of the gods,' is the indigenous spirituality of Japan, deeply interwoven with the nation's culture and its people's connection to nature. Unlike many world religions, Shinto does not have a founder or possess sacred scriptures akin to the Bible or Quran. Instead, it is characterized by its rituals, myriad kami (gods or spirits), and sacred shrines, which dot the Japanese landscape. Shinto's practices and beliefs reflect an intrinsic reverence for nature and ancestry, which is crucial in shaping Japanese identity and cultural practices.

The Pantheon of Kami

At the heart of Shinto are the kami, spirits that inhabit all things, animate and inanimate, infusing the natural world with divinity. The kami embody various aspects of nature and human values, from major deities like Amaterasu, the Sun Goddess considered the imperial family's progenitor, to local spirits associated with particular landscapes, trees, or waterfalls. The belief in kami underscores a world view that sees nature as alive, responsive, and worthy of respect and veneration.

Kami are not remote deities but integral to practitioners' daily lives; they are believed to influence everything from personal fortune to the harvest's success. This relationship is reciprocal; humans must honor the kami through rituals and offerings to maintain balance and harmony.

Sacred Shrines and Rituals

Shinto worship takes place at shrines (jinja), where the natural and the supernatural meet. Shrines can range from grand structures like the Ise Grand Shrine, which is dedicated to Amaterasu and rebuilt every twenty years in a centuries-old ritual of renewal, to small roadside entities housing local kami. These shrines are often located in places of natural beauty, reinforcing the bond between nature and spirituality that defines Shinto.

The rituals performed in Shinto, including purification rites, offerings of food and drink to the kami, and festivals (matsuri), are central to its practice. Purification, or harae, is particularly significant, involving cleansing pollution or sin from individuals, objects, or places through simple rites involving water, salt, or paper streamers. This purification allows practitioners and communities to renew their connection with the kami, ensuring their favor and benevolence.

Coexistence with Buddhism

Since its introduction to Japan in the 6th century, Buddhism has coexisted with Shinto in a complementary manner, influencing and being influenced by Shinto practices. This syncretism is evident in the seamless blend of religious practices seen in many Japanese lives; families may celebrate births and marriages with Shinto rites while honoring their ancestors and observing death rituals in a Buddhist context. Many religious sites in Japan even house both a Buddhist temple and a Shinto shrine, symbolically and physically representing this deep interrelation.

Influence on Japanese Culture and Traditions

Shinto's influence extends beyond religious practices into various aspects of Japanese culture, including art, literature, and national identity. Traditional arts like ikebana (flower arranging) and tea ceremonies reflect Shinto's emphasis on nature and meticulous attention to form, each act considered a gesture of respect towards the natural world.

Seasonal festivals and national holidays often have roots in Shinto, celebrating the rhythms of nature and the deeds of the kami. These public expressions of faith and tradition play a vital role in community bonding and transmitting cultural values from one generation to the next.

Shinto's pervasive influence on Japanese society and its cultural expressions showcases the profound depth of Japan's spiritual heritage. As a belief system, it teaches respect for nature, celebrates life's cyclical nature, and fosters a sense of belonging and continuity among the Japanese. In an age where the world grapples with ecological crises and questions of spiritual disconnect, Shinto offers a lens through which to view a harmonious interplay between humanity and the natural world, providing insights that resonate well beyond the archipelago of Japan.

Jainism: Ahimsa and Asceticism

Jainism, one of the world's oldest religions, presents a path deeply embedded in the principles of non-violence (ahimsa), asceticism, and ethical living. Arising in the same spiritual ferment of the Indian subcontinent that produced Buddhism, Jainism has maintained its distinct identity through a rigorous commitment to its core values, influencing millions of followers across generations to live lives of profound respect and care for all forms of life.

The Life of Mahavira

The historical trajectory of Jainism is often associated with Vardhamana Mahavira, a contemporary of Buddha and the last in a line of 24 Tirthankaras (spiritual teachers). Born into a noble family in the 6th century BCE, Mahavira, like Buddha, abandoned a life of luxury in search of spiritual truth. After 12 years of intense ascetic practices, including fasting, meditation, and enduring harsh physical conditions, Mahavira attained Kevala Jnana (omniscience). His enlightenment led to the formation of the principles that Jainism is known for today. Although Mahavira is not considered the founder of Jainism, his teachings form the core of current Jain philosophy.

Ahimsa: The Doctrine of Non-Violence

Central to Jainism is the doctrine of ahimsa, which goes beyond mere non-violence in action. Ahimsa in Jainism extends to thoughts and words, reflecting a holistic approach to peace and respect for life. Jains believe that every creature possesses a soul that is potentially divine; hence, harm towards any living being is considered harm towards oneself. This principle dictates many aspects of Jain life, from their strict vegetarianism to the wearing of masks by some sects to avoid inhaling insects, and gentle sweeping of the path in front of them to prevent stepping on living beings.

Asceticism and the Quest for Liberation

Ascetic practices are seen as a means to purify the soul and avoid karma which binds the soul to the cycle of birth and rebirth. Jains take up various vows of austerity, including fasting, renouncing material possessions, and leading a life of celibacy. These practices are more intense among Jain monks and nuns, but laypersons are also expected to observe less rigorous forms of asceticism.

The ultimate aim of these practices is moksha, or liberation from the cycle of birth, death, and rebirth. Moksha is achieved by freeing the soul from accumulated karma, allowing it to rise to its pure, original state and dwell at the top of the universe in perpetual bliss.

Self-Discipline and Community Ethics

Self-discipline in Jainism is not just about personal purity but is also about maintaining the ethical standards of the community. Jains often engage in practices such as Paryushan, a period of intense reflection, confession, and forgiveness. During this time, Jains may fast, meditate, and recite scriptures to purify themselves spiritually.

The community is also central to maintaining these rigorous standards. The Jain community is tightly-knit, with local temples serving as centers for learning and worship. The temple is where Jains engage in rituals that affirm their commitment to the five major vows: non-violence, truth, non-stealing, chastity, and non-attachment.

Vegetarianism and Environmental Responsibility

Vegetarianism in Jainism is a direct extension of ahimsa. Jains are strict vegetarians, and some are even vegan, avoiding all products derived from animals. This dietary choice is rooted in the desire to minimize harm to living beings, including animals and, in some interpretations, plants uprooted from the soil.

Moreover, Jainism's reverence for life extends to environmental ethics. Jains views nature as a living entity that is worthy of respect and protection. This perspective makes Jainism a deeply ecological religion, advocating for practices that protect the environment and ensure its sustainability.

Jainism offers a profound narrative on the potential for human beings to live in harmony with themselves and the world around them. Jainism prescribes a path to spiritual liberation through its teachings on non-violence, self-discipline, and asceticism. It promotes a way of life that is sustainable, ethical, and deeply respectful of life in all its forms. As humanity grapples with global challenges such as environmental degradation and social unrest, the Jain philosophy of peaceful coexistence and respect for life remains more relevant than ever, providing guiding principles for personal conduct and community ethics.

Sikhism: Unity of God and Equality of Mankind

Sikhism, a spiritual, social, and philosophical movement, originated in the Punjab region of South Asia during the 15th century under the guidance of Guru Nanak Dev Ji and was subsequently shaped by ten successive Gurus. This faith, while rooted in the historical context of religious conflict, introduced revolutionary ideas about the unity of God, the brotherhood of mankind, and the intrinsic equality of all human beings. These principles, deeply embedded in Sikh theology and practice, challenge social inequalities and advocate a life of devotion, honesty, and community service.

The Monotheistic Foundation

At the core of Sikh belief is the affirmation of a single, omnipotent, and omniscient God who transcends form, time, and space. Unlike many other religious traditions that portray God through various manifestations, Sikhism emphasizes the singularity and uniqueness of God with the opening phrase of the Guru Granth Sahib, the holy scripture of the Sikhs: "Ik Onkar" (One Universal Creator God). This declaration sets the stage for a profound understanding of divine presence that is immanent in all creation, accessible to everyone, and undivided by distinctions of creed, caste, or gender.

Guru Nanak and the Successive Sikh Gurus

Guru Nanak, the founder of Sikhism, expressed his divine experiences and insights through hymns and poems that emphasized the love of God, the futility of ritualism, and the importance of living a truthful and honest life. His teachings and those of the nine Gurus who succeeded him were compiled into the Guru Granth Sahib, which Sikhs consider their final and eternal Guru. This scripture not only contains the spiritual and moral guidance of the Sikh Gurus but also includes writings of Hindu and Muslim saints, underscoring the Sikh ethos of respect and inclusivity towards other faiths.

Equality and Social Justice

One of the most radical aspects of Sikhism is its staunch advocacy for social equality. From its inception, Sikhism has opposed the caste system, challenging the deeply ingrained social stratification of the Indian subcontinent. The institution of Langar, a communal meal served to all visitors of Sikh Gurdwaras (temples) without consideration of religion, caste, or social status, exemplifies this commitment. Initiated by Guru Nanak and institutionalized by Guru Amar Das, the third Sikh Guru, Langar serves as a practical demonstration of equality and the shared community life, which are central to Sikh practice.

Community and Military Spirit

The evolution of the Sikh community into a distinct religious and cultural identity was significantly shaped by the contributions of Guru Gobind Singh, the tenth Guru. In 1699, he founded the Khalsa, a community of the faithful who would be willing to lay down their lives to protect their faith and the oppressed. This military and spiritual order was characterized by specific codes of conduct and distinctive symbols known as the Five Ks: Kesh (uncut hair), Kara (a steel bracelet), Kanga (a wooden comb), Kachera (cotton undergarments), and Kirpan (a ceremonial sword). These symbols assert the believer's allegiance to their faith and their community responsibilities.

Modern Impact and Challenges

In the contemporary world, Sikhism is a vibrant faith with a global presence, advocating for peace, justice, and tolerance. However, Sikhs often face challenges such as misidentification and discrimination, particularly in international contexts where there is limited understanding of their faith. Despite these challenges, the community remains committed to the principles laid out by Guru Nanak and his successors, advocating for a world where religious harmony and human dignity can flourish.

Sikhism's emphasis on the unity of God and the equality of all persons offers a powerful counter-narrative to the divisions and disparities that afflict many societies today. By advocating a life of righteousness, selflessness, and social service, Sikhism provides spiritual guidance to its adherents and serves as a beacon of hope for universal brotherhood and peace. The enduring relevance of Sikh principles in addressing contemporary social issues underscores its potential as a transformative force in global ethical discourse. As Sikhism continues to grow and interact with diverse cultures and religions, its core values of faith, justice, and human solidarity remain as vital as ever, guiding adherents and inspiring communities towards greater understanding and cooperation.

Impact of Eastern Spirituality on Global Consciousness

In the tapestry of global spirituality, the threads of Eastern traditions have been interwoven deeply, influencing a broad spectrum of philosophical, religious, and practical aspects of life across the world. The profound concepts rooted in the philosophies of India, China, Japan, and other Eastern nations have transcended geographical boundaries, enriching global spirituality and reshaping Western perceptions on mind, body, and spirit. This article explores the multifaceted impact of these traditions, particularly through the widespread adoption of practices like meditation and yoga, the infusion of Eastern philosophy into Western thought, and the significant role Eastern traditions play in contemporary interfaith dialogues and spiritual practices.

The Global Spread of Meditation and Yoga

Meditation and yoga, ancient practices with their origins in Hindu and Buddhist traditions, have seen a meteoric rise in popularity across the globe. Meditation, as taught by Buddhist schools, emphasizes mindfulness and the cultivation of a calm, focused mind, free from the distractions of everyday life. This practice has been embraced widely in the West, particularly within the realms of psychology and therapy, where it is employed to reduce stress, anxiety, and depression, and to improve overall well-being.

Yoga, which encompasses a range of physical, mental, and spiritual practices, has similarly transcended its origins to become a global phenomenon. Rooted in the Hindu tradition and elaborated upon in texts like the Yoga Sutras of Patanjali, yoga in the Western world often focuses on postures (asanas) and breath control (pranayama), though its more profound spiritual and meditative aspects are increasingly recognized and practiced. The universal appeal of yoga lies in its adaptability; it offers physical health benefits while also providing pathways to spiritual mindfulness and discipline.

Influence on Western Thought

The 20th century witnessed an unprecedented openness in the West to Eastern philosophies, spurred by the works of thinkers like Alan Watts, who interpreted and disseminated Eastern spirituality through a contemporary Western lens. The philosophical and spiritual texts of Taoism and Buddhism, such as the *Tao Te Ching* and the teachings of Zen masters, have captivated Western intellectuals and spiritual seekers alike, offering alternative perspectives on existence, suffering, and enlightenment that challenge the traditionally dominant Judeo-Christian narrative.

Furthermore, the introduction of quantum physics and its exploration of the universe at the most microscopic levels has led to a surprising convergence with Eastern mystical concepts. The interconnectedness and impermanence that define quantum theory strikingly echo the principles found in Buddhism and Hinduism, fostering a dialogue between science and spirituality that continues to enrich both fields.

Role in Contemporary Interfaith Dialogues

Eastern spiritual traditions play a crucial role in contemporary interfaith dialogues, focusing on finding common ground among the world's major religions. The inclusive nature of Eastern philosophies, emphasising personal experience and inner transformation rather than dogmatic beliefs, makes them accessible to people of various faiths. These dialogues often explore concepts like compassion, non-attachment, and the pursuit of peace, which are central to Eastern traditions and resonate universally.

Buddhist concepts of compassion and non-violence have particularly influenced global peace and environmental movements, promoting a collective ethic of care that transcends religious and cultural divides. Similarly, the Jain principle of ahimsa (non-violence) has been echoed in movements for animal rights and non-violent protests, demonstrating the profound impact of these principles on global ethical practices.

The influence of Eastern spiritual traditions on global spirituality represents a significant cultural and philosophical exchange that has enriched global consciousness. By offering diverse methods of seeking understanding and enlightenment, Eastern traditions have broadened the spiritual horizons of millions worldwide. As globalization fosters greater interaction among diverse cultures, the continuing integration of Eastern spirituality into global practices promises to shape our collective spiritual landscape further, encouraging a deeper, more inclusive approach to understanding the mysteries of existence and the pursuit of harmony in an interconnected world.

Chapter 4: Western Traditions

Western spiritual traditions, with their rich tapestries of beliefs, rituals, and philosophical inquiries, have profoundly shaped the cultural, social, and moral landscapes of societies around the globe. This chapter delves into the intricate mosaic of religious thought that constitutes the Western spiritual heritage, exploring how Judaism, Christianity, Islam, and the philosophical currents of the European Enlightenment have each contributed to the development of Western civilization and influenced global spirituality.

The journey begins with Judaism, one of the oldest monotheistic religions, laying the foundational stones for Christianity and Islam. These Abrahamic faiths, though diverging in rituals and interpretations, share a common lineage that traces back to the ancient Near East. They have coexisted and interacted in complex ways throughout history, influencing art, science, politics, and philosophy across continents.

Christianity emerged from the Judaic roots and transformed the Roman Empire and established itself as a major cultural and political force. Its narratives, values, and liturgical practices have indelibly shaped Western art, music, literature, and law. The chapter will trace the evolution of Christianity from a persecuted sect to the state religion of the Roman Empire, through the schisms that led to the proliferation of various branches, and into its role in the modern world.

Although often associated primarily with the East, Islam has been a significant part of the Western religious landscape since its inception, especially in regions such as the Iberian Peninsula, the Balkans, and more recently in Western Europe. Its rich intellectual and cultural contributions during the Middle Ages were instrumental in shaping the Renaissance and the scientific advancements in Europe.

The European Enlightenment challenged the religious status quo by placing reason and empirical evidence at the center of human understanding. This intellectual revolution paved the way for modern secularism and continues to influence contemporary discussions on science, ethics, and governance.

Furthermore, this chapter will explore the rise of modern spiritual movements that reflect Western spirituality's dynamic and evolving nature in the contemporary world. These movements, from the revival of ancient pagan traditions to the emergence of new age spiritualities, highlight the ongoing quest for meaning and the continuous reinterpretation of the sacred in the modern context.

By exploring these diverse religious traditions and their interwoven impacts on Western society, this chapter aims to provide a comprehensive understanding of how spiritual thought in the West has navigated between reverence and reason, tradition and change, shaping Western identities and contributing to the global dialogue on spirituality. This exploration reflects on the past and offers insights into the evolving nature of spiritual life in the contemporary world, illustrating how ancient traditions continue to inform and respond to modern challenges.

Judaism: Covenant and Law

Judaism, one of the world's oldest monotheistic religions, has profoundly shaped humanity's spiritual and ethical landscape. Rooted in the covenantal relationship between the Hebrews and their God, this faith tradition has influenced countless aspects of culture, morality, and law across millennia. This article delves into the origins of Judaism, exploring its core beliefs centered around the covenant with Abraham, the profound significance of the Torah, and the religion's unique blend of prophetic traditions and legal ethics.

Judaism traces its origins back to the Bronze Age amidst the ancient civilizations of the Near East. Central to Jewish belief is the figure of Abraham, a patriarch whose life, as chronicled in the Hebrew Bible, marked the beginning of a distinct religious identity based on monotheism. The pivotal moment came when God promised Abraham that he would be the father of a great nation, a promise sealed with an everlasting covenant. This foundational relationship set the stage for the emergence of Judaism as a structured faith, influencing the development of two other major world religions, Christianity and Islam.

As the Israelites settled in Canaan and later when they formed the Kingdoms of Israel and Judah, the narrative of their trials, tribulations, and divine interactions were meticulously documented. These historical accounts provide not just the theological underpinnings of Judaism but also encapsulate the social and political challenges faced by the Jewish people throughout history.

At the heart of Judaism is the doctrine of monotheism, the belief in one, singular, omnipotent God. This was a revolutionary concept in a time when polytheistic religions dominated. The Jewish understanding of God as transcendent, yet personally involved in the world, set a new template for religious thought. God's laws were communicated through prophets—individuals chosen to deliver divine messages to the people. Prophets like Moses, Isaiah, and Jeremiah not only reinforced the covenantal relationship but also critiqued the moral failings of the community, calling for social justice, adherence to divine laws, and repentance.

The prophetic tradition emphasized that true piety was not merely ritualistic compliance but a commitment to righteousness, ethical behavior, and justice. This has imbued Jewish communities with a strong sense of moral purpose and social responsibility that resonates through the ages.

The Torah, encompassing the first five books of the Hebrew Bible, is the cornerstone of Jewish life and law. Regarded as the direct word of God as revealed to Moses on Mount Sinai, the Torah provides detailed instructions on religious observance, ethical conduct, and social law. Its commandments (mitzvot) govern all aspects of life, from dietary restrictions and principles of charity to guidelines for worship and personal conduct.

The legalistic detail of the Torah is further explored and interpreted through the Talmud, a comprehensive written version of the Jewish oral law. The interpretation of these texts is a dynamic process, giving rise to a rich tradition of rabbinical commentary and legal debate that adapts Jewish law to the changing conditions of society, illustrating the dynamic and living nature of Jewish law.

Judaism's emphasis on law, ethical monotheism, and social justice has profoundly impacted the West's religious and cultural development. Jewish texts and concepts deeply influenced Christian theology, as Christianity emerged from within the Jewish community. The ethical monotheism of Judaism provided a scaffold that supported the development of Western legal systems and moral philosophy.

Judaism's historical journey from the ancient covenant with Abraham to the elaboration of its laws and prophetic traditions reveals a deeply traditional and adaptive religion. Its profound emphasis on community, justice, and ethical monotheism continues to inspire and challenge followers and non-followers alike. As one of the foundational pillars of Western spirituality, Judaism survives and thrives, continually influencing the moral compass of societies and fostering a deep, enduring sense of identity and purpose among the Jewish people.

Christianity: Faith and Universalism

Christianity, originating as a modest Jewish sect, has evolved over two millennia into a global faith with profound influence on the cultural, philosophical, and political landscapes of societies worldwide. This article traces the historical and theological journey of Christianity, exploring its foundational doctrines, the pivotal role of the early church and apostles, and the significant councils and schisms that shaped its diverse denominations.

Christianity began in the 1st century AD in the Roman province of Judea, with the teachings and life events of Jesus of Nazareth at its core. Jesus' ministry, crucifixion, and subsequent resurrection are the foundational pillars of Christian doctrine, marking a new covenant between God and humanity. Central to Christian belief are the doctrines of the Incarnation—God becoming flesh in the person of Jesus Christ—and the Resurrection, which asserts Jesus' victory over death and his divine nature.

His disciples preserved and disseminated these events and Jesus' teachings, who interpreted his message as a universal call to salvation, transcending Jewish law and reaching out to Gentiles (non-Jews). This universalism was a pivotal development, facilitated by key figures such as the Apostle Paul, whose missionary journeys and extensive writings helped establish early Christian communities across the Roman Empire.

The early church's development was marked by its communal ethos and adherence to the teachings of Jesus and his immediate followers, the apostles. The apostolic era is characterized by the spread of the

Gospel and the establishment of churches from Jerusalem to as far as Rome and Alexandria. During this formative period, the church faced external persecutions and internal heresies, which prompted the need for formal doctrinal and organizational structures.

As disputes over Christ's divine and human natures threatened unity, church leaders convened councils to standardize Christian doctrine. The First Council of Nicaea in 325 AD, convened by Emperor Constantine, addressed the Arian controversy regarding the nature of Christ's divinity. The Nicene Creed, established there, affirmed the Son's co-eternity and consubstantiality with the Father, laying a foundational orthodoxy for future generations.

The Council of Chalcedon in 451 AD further refined these doctrines by describing the dual nature of Christ—fully divine and fully human. These ecumenical councils were instrumental in defining orthodox Christian theology and in fortifying the church's structure and reach across the Empire.

The first major schism in Christianity occurred in 1054, known as the Great Schism, which divided the church into the Roman Catholic Church in the West and the Orthodox Church in the East. This split was rooted in both theological disputes—such as the source of the Holy Spirit and the use of unleavened bread in the Eucharist—and political conflicts between the Eastern Byzantine and the Western Roman empires.

Later, in the 16th century, the Protestant Reformation led by figures like Martin Luther and John Calvin challenged the authority and practices of the Catholic Church, leading to the formation of various Protestant denominations. These reforms emphasized doctrines such as justification by faith alone and the authority of the Scriptures over church tradition, significantly altering Europe's religious, cultural, and political landscape.

Each branch of Christianity—Catholic, Orthodox, and Protestant—has developed distinct theological emphases and cultural expressions which have deeply influenced global arts, sciences, and philosophies. Christianity's moral and ethical teachings have shaped laws and societal norms, its rich tradition of theological and philosophical thought has fostered dialogue and intellectual development, and its commitment to social justice and charity has had a lasting impact on global humanitarian efforts.

From its humble beginnings in Judea to its status as a world religion, Christianity's journey is one of profound transformation and enduring influence. Through its teachings, its community's resilience, and its adaptability to diverse cultures, Christianity plays a crucial role in shaping individual lives and global civilizations, offering a message of hope, redemption, and universal love.

Islam: Revelation and Community

Islam, the youngest of the major Abrahamic religions, has profoundly shaped the religious, cultural, and political landscapes of vast regions across the globe. From the life and revelations of Prophet Muhammad to the rich contributions of the Islamic Golden Age, this faith has offered a unique blend of spirituality, community life, and intellectual pursuit. This article explores the foundational aspects of Islam, its doctrinal core, the formation of its community, and its expansive influence on world civilizations.

Islam's origins trace back to the 7th century in the Arabian city of Mecca, where Prophet Muhammad, a then forty-year-old merchant, began to receive revelations from God through the angel Gabriel. These revelations, which continued for over two decades, were compiled into the Qur'an, the holy book of Islam, which Muslims consider the literal word of God and the final testament in a series of divine messages sent through earlier prophets including Abraham, Moses, and Jesus.

Muhammad's mission went beyond mere proclamation; he sought to radically transform his society by reforming its morals, social customs, and religious beliefs. His teachings emphasized monotheism, social justice, and moral rectitude. As the Qur'an's recitations spread, Muhammad gathered a growing number of followers, forming the nascent Muslim community.

The core framework of Islamic practice is built around the Five Pillars, which outline the essential acts of worship and conduct that define a Muslim's faith and practices. These are the shahada (declaration of faith), which asserts the oneness of God and the prophethood of Muhammad; salat (prayer), performed five times a day; zakat (almsgiving), a form of wealth redistribution to assist the less fortunate; sawm (fasting during Ramadan), a month of fasting from dawn to sunset to cultivate piety and empathy for the impoverished; and hajj (pilgrimage to Mecca), required once in a lifetime for those who are physically and financially able.

After Muhammad's death in 632 AD, Islam spread rapidly beyond the Arabian Peninsula under the leadership of his successors, the Caliphs. By the end of the 8th century, the Islamic empire extended from Spain in the west to the borders of India in the east, making it one of the largest empires in history. This expansion facilitated the exchange of ideas, cultures, and knowledge between diverse peoples.

The Islamic community, however, was not without internal conflict, particularly the major sectarian split into Sunni and Shia Islam, primarily stemming from disagreements over the rightful successor to Muhammad. Sunni Islam, which forms the majority, believes in the elected caliphate, while Shia Islam holds that leadership should stay within the Prophet's family, starting with his cousin and son-in-law, Ali. This division has had deep religious, cultural, and political implications throughout Islamic history.

The period from the 8th to the 14th century, often referred to as the Islamic Golden Age, was marked by monumental advancements in science, medicine, mathematics, and philosophy. Muslim scholars, such as Al-Khwarizmi in mathematics, Ibn Sina in medicine, and Al-Farabi in philosophy, made significant contributions that would later find their way to Europe and have a lasting impact on the Renaissance and beyond.

Islamic civilization also excelled in arts, architecture, and literature, with exquisite developments in calligraphy, tilework, and poetry, which have immensely contributed to the cultural richness of regions extending from the Middle East to Southeast Asia.

Islam's comprehensive approach to life, which integrates spirituality with social responsibility, learning, and ethics, continues to resonate across the world. As it interacts with modernity, Islam remains a dynamic force, shaping and reshaping the lives of its followers and influencing global cultural, intellectual, and religious landscapes. Its rich heritage, profound on both spiritual and intellectual levels, continues to foster dialogue and interaction across diverse global communities.

The European Enlightenment

The European Enlightenment, a pivotal movement spanning the 17th and 18th centuries, marked a profound shift in the way humanity understood itself and the world. Characterized by an audacious spirit of inquiry, the Enlightenment championed reason, individualism, and skepticism of traditional authority, particularly in matters of religion and governance. This intellectual awakening questioned long-held dogmas and laid the groundwork for modern secular societies. This article explores the contributions of key Enlightenment thinkers, their impact on the development of secularism, and the enduring influence on Western thought and society.

The Enlightenment era, often referred to as the Age of Reason, emerged as a response to the perceived inadequacies of religious and monarchical authority which had dominated Europe for centuries. Philosophers and scientists began to advocate for the use of reason as the best means of understanding reality and addressing human problems. This radical shift proposed that humanity could achieve progress and enlightenment through empirical evidence and logical thought, rather than relying on religious or royal decree.

Immanuel Kant, a central figure of the Enlightenment, famously encapsulated the ethos of the period in his rallying cry: "Sapere aude" ("Dare to know"). Kant argued that individuals should exercise their reason without the guidance of another. His critical philosophy, especially his notion of the 'categorical imperative,' reshaped ethics by insisting that moral principles should be universal and applicable independently of religious considerations.

Voltaire, one of the era's most prolific writers, used his sharp wit to criticize the Church and the absolutism of the French monarchy. His advocacy for religious tolerance, freedom of speech, and reason made him influential in the movement towards secular governance.

Jean-Jacques Rousseau diverged somewhat in his focus on human nature's emotional and social aspects but was equally transformative. Rousseau's concept of the "social contract" proposed that legitimate political authority rests not with kings or gods but with the general will of the people, an idea that profoundly influenced the democratic revolutions of the late 18th century.

The Enlightenment facilitated the rise of secularism by challenging the intertwining of church and state that had characterized European nations. Philosophers and thinkers argued that ethical and moral decisions could be governed by human reason and natural law rather than religious doctrine. This shift affected religious institutions and transformed political ones, leading to the development of structures that promote governmental accountability and individual rights.

The intellectual currents set in motion by the Enlightenment have had lasting effects on Western society and thought. The emphasis on scientific inquiry and skepticism has fostered continued progress in technology and science. The focus on individual rights and justice informed the development of modern liberal democracies and the universal declaration of human rights. Moreover, the secularism that emerged from Enlightenment thought has created societies that uphold the freedom of religion, allowing a pluralism of beliefs and ideas that continue to enrich Western cultures.

The European Enlightenment remains one of the most influential periods in human history, with its ideals continuing to underpin much of Western thought and democratic ideology. The Enlightenment philosophers sought to liberate humanity from unexamined obedience and foster a world more reliant on inquiry and less on dogma by championing reason over tradition and individualism over collective authority. As contemporary societies continue to grapple with issues of ethics, governance, and the role of religion in public life, the lessons of the Enlightenment are as relevant today as they were two centuries ago.

Contemporary Spiritual Movements in the West

In recent decades, the spiritual landscape of the Western world has undergone a significant transformation, marked by a shift away from traditional religious affiliations towards a more eclectic and personalized approach to spirituality. This shift has given rise to a variety of contemporary spiritual movements, including New Age philosophies, the resurgence of Neopaganism, and a broad interest in non-traditional spiritual practices. These movements reflect deeper changes in Western attitudes towards religion and a growing desire for spiritual experiences that are personal, direct, and unmediated by institutional frameworks.

New Age Movements: A Synthesis of Eclectic Spiritual Practices

New Age movements, which gained prominence in the late 20th century, are characterized by their eclectic approach to spirituality. Drawing from Eastern religions, mysticism, esoteric traditions, and even quantum physics, New Age thought typically emphasizes the interconnectedness of all life, personal empowerment, and a holistic approach to health and well-being. Central to New Age philosophy is the belief in a new era of consciousness—referred to as the "Age of Aquarius"—which is said to bring about a profound transformation in human potential and awareness.

New Age practices include meditation, astrology, crystal healing, energy medicine, and channeling. These practices are often individualized and geared towards self-improvement, self-healing, and a deeper understanding of one's own place in the cosmos. The popularity of these practices reflects a broader trend towards spirituality that is not only personalized but also integrated into daily life outside traditional religious settings.

Resurgence of Neopaganism: Reconnecting with Ancient Traditions

Neopaganism represents another significant trend in contemporary Western spirituality. This movement seeks to revive and reinterpret pre-Christian, often polytheistic religious traditions, including those of ancient Europe. Modern Pagan groups such as Wiccans, Druids, and followers of Asatru draw inspiration from old myths, rituals, and beliefs, adapting them to modern contexts and sensibilities.

Central to Neopaganism is a strong emphasis on nature worship and environmental awareness, reflecting concerns about the modern disconnection from the natural world and ecological degradation. Ritual practices often celebrate the cycles of nature, such as solstices, equinoxes, and phases of the moon, which are seen as manifestations of the divine. The growth of Neopaganism can be seen as part of a broader spiritual ecology movement, which emphasizes living in harmony with the earth as a conscious spiritual practice.

Non-Traditional Spiritual Practices: The Quest for Authentic Experience

The turn towards non-traditional spiritual practices is often motivated by a search for authenticity and direct personal experience of the divine. Many individuals in the West are drawn to practices that offer immediate, experiential engagement with spirituality, such as mindfulness, yoga, shamanic journeying, or transcendental meditation. These practices often promise spiritual enlightenment and mental and physical health benefits, appealing to the modern individual's desire for practical spirituality that enhances everyday life.

Furthermore, these practices frequently involve a component of community and shared experience, reflecting a shift from solitary religious observance to more communal forms of spiritual engagement. Spiritual retreats, workshops, and festivals provide spaces where individuals can explore their spirituality in a supportive community setting.

The rise of contemporary spiritual movements in the West can be seen as a response to the perceived limitations of organized religion, particularly its ability to meet individuals' personal and immediate spiritual needs. As Western societies become more pluralistic and individualized, these movements offer new ways of understanding the self and the universe, proposing a more fluid and customizable approach to spirituality. This trend towards eclectic, non-traditional spiritual practices suggests a continuing evolution of the spiritual landscape, where personal experience and exploration take precedence over adherence to established religious doctrines. As such, contemporary spiritual movements are likely to play an increasingly significant role in shaping the future of Western spirituality, reflecting ongoing changes in how people relate to the sacred in an increasingly complex world.

Interfaith Dialogue and Religious Pluralism

In an increasingly interconnected and multicultural world, the religious landscape of Western societies has become notably diverse. This diversity has prompted significant reflection within religious communities, leading to a concerted effort to engage in interfaith dialogue and promote religious pluralism. These initiatives are not

Elena Ray

merely academic or theological exercises; they are vital responses to the realities of global migration, cultural exchange, and the quest for social harmony in pluralistic societies. This article explores the complexities of interfaith dialogue, the opportunities it presents, and the challenges religious communities face in embracing pluralism.

The Rise of Interfaith Dialogue

Interfaith dialogue involves open, respectful discussions between people of different religious and spiritual backgrounds. It aims to increase understanding and cooperation by highlighting commonalities, such as shared values and ethical standards, while also acknowledging and respecting religious differences. In Western countries, where secularism and a multitude of religious traditions coexist, interfaith dialogue has become increasingly important.

Organizations dedicated to fostering such dialogues have sprung up in numerous cities across Europe and North America. These range from local interfaith councils that organize community events to international bodies that promote peace and cooperation between large religious institutions. Notable among these is the Parliament of the World's Religions, which provides a global forum for addressing issues like peace, environmental sustainability, and human rights from diverse religious perspectives.

Promoting Religious Pluralism

Religious pluralism goes beyond mere tolerance of different religious practices and seeks to understand and celebrate the richness that religious diversity brings to society. This approach helps reduce religious discrimination and prejudice and enhances the social cohesion of increasingly diverse populations. In promoting pluralism, religious communities and leaders play a crucial role in shaping attitudes towards inclusivity and mutual respect.

Educational initiatives play a pivotal role in this regard. Many religious and educational institutions now offer programs that educate the youth about the beliefs and practices of different world religions, aiming to cultivate a foundation of respect and understanding from an early age.

Challenges of Religious Diversity

There are notable challenges despite the positive intentions and significant benefits of interfaith dialogue and religious pluralism. One of the primary challenges is the resistance within more conservative or traditionalist segments of religious communities. For some, engaging in dialogue with other faiths may be seen as compromising their own religious truths or diluting their faith's teachings.

Furthermore, political and social tensions can exacerbate religious differences, turning benign theological disagreements into sources of conflict. In some Western societies, the rise of nationalist movements has been linked with increased xenophobia, which can include religious intolerance. This creates a hostile environment for interfaith dialogue, which relies on openness and trust.

Opportunities Presented by Religious Diversity

Despite these challenges, the opportunities arising from religious diversity and interfaith dialogue are significant. Such engagements not only help alleviate misconceptions and stereotypes but also enrich participants' spiritual lives. Many who engage in interfaith activities report a deeper understanding of their faiths through explaining their beliefs to others and encountering alternative viewpoints.

Moreover, collaborative efforts between different religious groups have proven effective in addressing global challenges such as poverty, climate change, and peacemaking. The shared commitment to humanitarian values can lead to powerful alliances that transcend religious boundaries, showcasing the potential for unified action in a fragmented world.

Interfaith dialogue and the promotion of religious pluralism represent crucial avenues for building more inclusive and harmonious societies. As Western nations continue to navigate the complexities of globalization and cultural diversification, the willingness of religious communities to engage in open dialogue and embrace pluralistic values will be key to fostering mutual understanding and peace. In doing so, these communities contribute to the social fabric of their societies and set a precedent for global cooperation in an increasingly interconnected world.

Chapter 5: Indigenous and Pagan Traditions

In the diverse and intricate landscape of global spirituality, indigenous and Pagan traditions occupy a unique and profound space. Rooted deeply in the natural world and often predating more formalized religious systems, these traditions offer a window into humanity's earliest attempts to understand and articulate its place within the cosmos. Chapter 5 delves into the rich spiritual life of indigenous peoples across various continents and the resurgence of Pagan traditions that seek to reconnect with ancient practices.

Indigenous spiritualities, from the Native American tribes of North America to the Aboriginal communities of Australia, share common themes of connection to land, community rituals, and a holistic view of existence where every element of the natural world holds spiritual significance. These traditions are not relics of the past but are living, breathing practices that continue to evolve and adapt to contemporary challenges while maintaining their distinct cultural identities.

Simultaneously, the chapter explores modern Paganism, a movement that has gained momentum in the West over the past century. This renaissance of ancient European spiritual practices, such as Wicca, Druidry, and Heathenry, reflects a growing desire to return to a more direct, personal experience of the sacred through rituals, celebrations of the natural cycles, and polytheistic worship.

As we journey through the beliefs, rituals, and cultural significances of these traditions, we confront the diversity of spiritual expression and the universal human themes of belonging, identity, and the quest for meaning. These traditions challenge the dominant paradigms of spirituality and invite a broader understanding of the sacred, emphasizing sustainability, respect for nature, and the interdependence of life.

This chapter aims to highlight both the historical depth and the contemporary relevance of indigenous and Pagan traditions. It examines how these spiritual paths have contributed to cultural richness and ecological awareness, providing valuable insights into how we might live more harmoniously within the larger community of life on Earth.

Overview of Indigenous Spirituality

Indigenous spirituality encompasses many beliefs and practices rooted in the deep connection between communities and their natural environments. Unlike the monotheistic or dogma-driven religions that have often dominated global narratives, indigenous spiritual practices are profoundly local, interwoven with the people's lore, landscape, and life. This article explores the diverse expressions of indigenous spirituality across various regions—North America, the Arctic, Sub-Saharan Africa, Australia, and the Pacific Islands— while highlighting common themes such as a deep connection to the land, animism, and community-centric rituals.

North American Indigenous Spirituality

In North America, indigenous spirituality varies significantly among tribes, yet common elements often include a profound respect for nature and animal spirits. The spiritual practices of tribes such as the Navajo, Lakota, and Iroquois emphasize harmony with the earth, seen in rituals that mark the cycles of nature, from planting to harvest. Totem poles of the Pacific Northwest embody the spiritual and familial heritage of peoples, telling stories of mystical creatures and clan ancestry, while the Sun Dance, a communal ritual among the Plains tribes, seeks to renew the world's vitality.

Arctic Spiritual Practices

The harsh environment of the Arctic has shaped the spiritual outlook of its indigenous peoples, such as the Inuit and Saami. Their spirituality is deeply tied to the land and its creatures, particularly marine animals that are vital to their subsistence. Shamanism plays a crucial role in Arctic spirituality, with shamans mediating between humans and the spirit world to ensure successful hunts and community welfare. The animistic belief system imbues animals and elements—ice, wind, and snow—with spiritual essence.

Sub-Saharan African Spirituality

Sub-Saharan Africa hosts a rich mosaic of tribal religions, each with its unique spiritual system yet commonly linked by animism and ancestor worship. Rituals and ceremonies are often presided over by a shaman or priest, believed to possess the ability to communicate with the spirit world, including ancestors who play an active role in the community's daily life. The rituals frequently involve music and dance, which are vital for maintaining the balance between the physical and spiritual worlds.

Australian Aboriginal Spirituality

For Australian Aboriginals, the Dreamtime is the foundation of life and spirituality. It explains the creation of the universe and governs the laws of community living and individual responsibility. The spiritual connection to the land is encapsulated in the concept of "country," which is considered a living entity, rich with cultural stories and spiritual significance. Sacred sites dot the landscape as nexuses of spiritual energy and communal memory.

Pacific Island Spirituality

In the vast expanse of the Pacific, islands like Hawaii, Fiji, and Aotearoa (New Zealand) have developed unique and interconnected spiritualities, with the ocean playing a central role. Navigational skills, for instance, were practical necessities and sacred arts, guided by stars, ocean swells, and wildlife patterns. The concept of mana (spiritual energy or power) is prevalent, often associated with gods of volcanoes, the sea, and the sky, reflecting the Islanders' deep respect for the forces of nature that shape their world.

Common Themes in Indigenous Spirituality

Across these diverse regions, several themes resonate deeply. The connection to the land is not merely utilitarian but spiritual, where landforms and elements of the natural world are imbued with sacred significance. Animism is another pervasive element, reflecting a worldview in which all things—animal, plant, and mineral—are endowed with a spiritual essence. Finally, community-focused rituals underscore the collective aspect of indigenous spiritualities, serving both religious functions and social and educational purposes, reinforcing bonds within the community and across generations.

Indigenous spirituality remains a vital, living practice that adapts while maintaining a continuity with the past. As the world grapples with questions of environmental sustainability and cultural preservation, the spiritual traditions of indigenous peoples offer insights into living in balance with the natural world. Their rich spiritual heritage, with its emphasis on interconnectedness and reverence for nature, provides a window into a profound way of seeing the world and essential lessons for the global community on the stewardship of the earth.

Native American Spirituality

Native American spirituality encompasses a profound diversity of beliefs and practices, reflecting the rich cultural tapestries of the various tribes that span the North American continent. Central to these traditions are a deep reverence for the natural world and a robust lineage of rituals, storytelling, and dance, which serve spiritual purposes, strengthen communal ties, and ensure the preservation of ancestral wisdom. This article delves into the spiritual world of Native American communities, highlighting key practices such as the worship of the Great Spirit, totemism, vision quests, and the use of sweat lodges, while exploring how storytelling and dance play crucial roles in these rich cultural expressions.

The Great Spirit and Totemism

Among the most profound elements in Native American spiritual practice is the belief in the Great Spirit, a supreme entity that embodies the sacredness of the universe. This belief is not uniform but manifests differently across tribes, reflecting various attributes of the Great Spirit, from creator to protector, that resonate with the tribe's environment and history. This overarching spirituality is deeply animistic, viewing all elements of nature—animals, plants, rivers, and mountains—as living, breathing entities imbued with spirit.

Totemism is another significant aspect of Native American spirituality, particularly prominent among tribes in the Pacific Northwest, such as the Haida and Tlingit. Totems are often depicted as animal spirits or ancestor spirits carved into towering totem poles, serving both as emblems of tribal lineage and as a medium through which stories and societal values are passed down. These totems are not mere symbols but are considered kin, with whom tribe members share a profound spiritual connection and responsibility.

Elena Ray

Vision Quests and Sweat Lodges

Vision quests are a pivotal rite of passage for many Native American youths, especially among the Plains tribes such as the Lakota and Blackfoot. This solitary journey into the wilderness seeks spiritual guidance and a vision of one's life purpose from the spirit world. Undertaken at a pivotal moment in a young person's life, the vision quest underscores the deep connection between individual identity and cosmic destiny, facilitated through intense prayer, fasting, and exposure to the elements.

Similarly, sweat lodges are used across many tribes as a purification ritual that symbolizes rebirth. Constructed from natural materials, these dome-shaped enclosures serve as the womb of Mother Earth. Participants enter to sweat out physical and spiritual impurities through prayers, chants, and the intense heat generated by hot stones. This purification process is considered essential for spiritual clarity and physical health.

Storytelling and Dance

Storytelling and dance are integral to Native American spiritual practices, serving as entertainment and more profoundly as spiritual education and community bonding. Elders often tell stories and are replete with teachings about the spiritual, social, and natural laws that govern the tribe. They are a living archive of the tribe's history, cosmology, and moral values.

Dance, too, is a powerful expression of Native American spirituality, used in ceremonies to invoke spirits, heal the sick, or call for rain. Dances like the Ghost Dance or the Sun Dance are highly symbolic, performed with specific regalia and movements that are believed to harness spiritual power. Through dance, participants step into a liminal space where they can interact with the spirit world, appealing to the ancestors and gods to intervene in their lives.

The spiritual traditions of Native American tribes offer a window into a world where every element of existence is interconnected through the sacred web of life. The rituals, stories, and dances of these tribes are not relics of the past but are vibrant, living expressions of a spiritual heritage that continues to evolve while maintaining its profound connections to the earth and the ancestral past. As modern challenges threaten these traditions, understanding and respecting their depth and significance is crucial for their preservation and enrichment of global cultural diversity and spiritual empathy.

Aboriginal Australian Beliefs

The spiritual traditions of Australian Aboriginals offer a profound window into one of the oldest continuous cultures on Earth. At the heart of these traditions lies the Dreamtime, a complex network of creation stories, spiritual lore, and laws that govern everything from social behavior to interactions with the natural world. This article delves into the intricacies of the Dreamtime, explores the pivotal role of songlines in Aboriginal spirituality, and reflects on how these elements combine to guide the cultural identity and practices of Aboriginal communities.

The Dreamtime transcends the concept of "time" in Western paradigms. It refers to both a time long past when ancestral spirits roamed the earth, shaping its landscapes and creating its various creatures, and a timeless time that continues to permeate the present, influencing every aspect of Aboriginal life. These ancestral beings, often depicted as half-human and half-animal, embarked on epic journeys across the land, their actions and interactions creating the physical features of the landscape and establishing the cultural laws that still resonate today.

The narratives of the Dreamtime are not merely myths or folklore; they are integral to the moral and legal systems of Aboriginal communities. They dictate the rules of kinship, marriage, and community responsibilities, serving as the bedrock of social order and spiritual health. These stories are passed down through generations in various forms—songs, dances, art, and ceremonial rituals—ensuring their survival and continual relevance.

One of the most remarkable aspects of Aboriginal spirituality is the system of songlines, also known as Dreaming tracks. Songlines are paths across the land (or sometimes the sky) that mark the route the creator-beings took as they made the world. These paths are recorded in songs, stories, dances, and paintings that recount the creation saga and the lore associated with specific locales.

Songlines serve multiple functions within Aboriginal culture. They are navigational tools that guide physical travel across the continent, connecting distant communities and sacred sites. More profoundly, they are spiritual conduits that offer paths to the deeper understanding of the world and the forces that animate it. By singing the songs or recounting the stories of a songline, individuals can invoke the power and presence of the ancestral spirits associated with those places.

The link between the land and Aboriginal identity is inseparable and sacred. The land is not just a source of sustenance; it is imbued with spiritual significance, holding the power and essence of the Dreamtime itself. Every mountain, river, rock, and tree has its story, spirit, and place within the broader cosmology. The profound connection to the land shapes the cultural practices and spiritual life of Aboriginal communities, emphasizing a stewardship that is based on respect and reciprocity.

While Aboriginal spirituality has endured for thousands of years, it faces contemporary challenges that threaten its transmission and practice. Issues such as land rights, the disruption of traditional ways of life, and the impact of modern Australian society pose significant threats. In response, Aboriginal leaders and communities are actively involved in efforts to preserve their heritage, advocating for legal recognition of their land rights, and finding new ways to share and celebrate their ancestral knowledge in a changing world.

The spiritual traditions of Australian Aboriginals provide not only a lens into a rich and ancient heritage but also universal lessons on the interconnectedness of life and the importance of living in harmony with the environment. The Dreamtime and the system of songlines offer more than historical insight; they present a living, breathing philosophy that emphasizes balance, respect, and the cyclical nature of life. As such, these traditions are vital to their cultural preservation and the global dialogue on sustainability and spiritual plurality.

Sub-Saharan African Religions

Sub-Saharan Africa, a region of immense cultural and ecological diversity, is home to a rich mosaic of religious beliefs that have shaped the identities and worldviews of its many peoples. Far from being monolithic, the spiritual traditions across this vast area are as varied as the landscapes in which they are practiced. From the worship of ancestors to the veneration of natural spirits and the vibrant rituals that celebrate this connection, these religious practices are deeply woven into the fabric of daily life and community cohesion.

Ancestral worship stands as a cornerstone of many African religious systems, reflecting a profound respect for the elders and forebears of the community. In cultures ranging from the Yoruba in the west to the Zulu in the south, ancestors are revered not merely as remembrances of the past but as active participants in the present, influencing the lives of the living through guidance, protection, and sometimes retribution. Rituals to honor ancestors are integral, involving offerings, prayers, and specific ceremonies designed to maintain their goodwill and seek their advice. This reverence ensures that the wisdom of the past is continuously integrated into the living community, fostering a sense of continuity and spiritual responsibility among its members.

Masks and drums feature prominently in the religious ceremonies of many Sub-Saharan African communities, serving as vital tools for communication with the spiritual world. Masks are often crafted to represent spirits, ancestors, or mythological beings and are worn during rituals to embody these powers. The use of masks can transform a participant into a vessel for the spirit, allowing them to communicate divine messages or healing powers to the community. This transformation is further facilitated by the rhythm of the drums, which are believed to summon spirits and generate the energy necessary to bridge the earthly and the divine.

In societies like the Dogon of Mali or the Bwa of Burkina Faso, masks and drums are not merely cultural artifacts but are imbued with sacred power. They play a crucial role in initiation rites, seasonal festivals, and healing ceremonies, where they help to align the community with the spiritual forces that govern their world.

The belief in spirits associated with natural features such as trees, rivers, mountains, and even certain animals is prevalent across Sub-Saharan Africa. These spirits are often seen as guardians of the environment and are integral to the ecological and spiritual health of the area. For instance, the Serer people of Senegal maintain sacred groves, untouched parts of the forest where the earth spirits reside, and where community members can go to seek healing or spiritual encounters.

These natural spirits require respect and veneration, and rituals to honor them are designed to ensure harmony between human activities and the natural world. This symbiotic relationship is vital for the community's survival, as it aligns agricultural and hunting practices with spiritual and ecological principles, promoting sustainability and respect for the earth.

Religious practices in Sub-Saharan Africa are not confined to specific holy places or times but permeate everyday life, influencing everything from judicial decisions and conflict resolution to agricultural practices and family life. Rituals and religious observances are communal activities that strengthen social bonds and reinforce community norms and values.

Moreover, the oral transmission of religious lore through stories, songs, and dances ensures that these practices are accessible to all community members, creating a shared repository of knowledge and spiritual wisdom that supports community cohesion and continuity.

The religious traditions of Sub-Saharan Africa offer a dynamic and integrated approach to spirituality that underscores the interconnection of community, the natural world, and the spiritual realm. These practices foster a deep sense of belonging and responsibility among individuals, linking them to their community, environment, and history through a shared spiritual heritage. As such, they provide a framework for understanding the world and practical guidelines for living within it harmoniously, making these traditions both timeless and profoundly relevant in the modern world.

Spirituality in the Andes and Amazon

The spiritual landscapes of the Andean highlands and the Amazon rainforest are as diverse and complex as their ecosystems. Rooted deeply in the land, these traditions encompass a wide array of practices, beliefs, and rituals that reflect the indigenous peoples' intimate connection with nature. This article explores two significant aspects: the worship of Pachamama, or Mother Earth, in the Andes, and the shamanistic traditions involving ayahuasca in the Amazon, illustrating how these spiritual practices form a fundamental part of cultural identity and ecological understanding.

Worship of Pachamama in the Andean Highlands

In the Andean regions of South America, spanning countries like Peru, Bolivia, and Ecuador, Pachamama is revered as a benevolent deity symbolizing fertility, harvest, and the earth itself. This veneration of Mother Earth is an ancient practice, deeply embedded in the daily lives of the Andean people. Pachamama is not only a spiritual entity but also a representation of nature's generative powers, crucial for agriculture in the challenging terrains of the Andes.

Rituals dedicated to Pachamama are particularly prominent during the sowing and harvesting seasons, when communities come together to seek her blessings for a bountiful yield. Offerings, known as "despacho," are common and involve burying or burning a collection of symbolic items such as coca leaves, grains, and figurines. These offerings are meant to appease Pachamama, ensuring her goodwill and fertility in the coming seasons.

The Use of Coca Leaves in Rituals

Coca leaves, which are native to the Andean region, hold profound cultural and spiritual significance beyond their infamous derivative, cocaine. For the indigenous communities, coca is sacred, used not only as a mild stimulant but also in various rituals. Chewing coca leaves is a traditional method to connect with the spiritual world, gain endurance, and mitigate hunger and altitude sickness.

In rituals, shamans often read coca leaves to divine the future or diagnose health, social, or spiritual issues within the community. These leaves are also presented as offerings to other deities and spirits, including the mountain spirits, or Apus, which are considered guardians of the people and their environments.

Shamanistic Traditions of the Amazonian Tribes

Moving from the high Andes to the dense Amazon, the spiritual practices shift to the rich shamanistic traditions that center around the use of ayahuasca, a potent hallucinogenic brew. Derived from the Banisteriopsis caapi vine and other ingredients, ayahuasca is used primarily for spiritual healing and divination, facilitating deep, visionary experiences that are said to connect individuals with the spiritual world.

Shamans, or curanderos, administer ayahuasca in carefully prepared ceremonies that are integral to many indigenous cultures in the Amazon. Participants in these ceremonies often seek healing for physical, emotional, or spiritual ailments, guidance in life decisions, or cleansing from bad spirits. The intense experiences induced by ayahuasca are believed to open up pathways to the spiritual realm, allowing shamans to communicate with spirits, diagnose the root causes of maladies, and restore balance to affected individuals.

Integration into Daily Life and Community Cohesion

Both in the Andes and the Amazon, spirituality is not segregated from daily life but is a fundamental component that sustains individual and communal existence. These practices foster a strong sense of community, as shared rituals and beliefs knit individuals tightly together and create a collective identity that respects and revolves around the natural world.

The spiritual traditions of the Andean highlands and the Amazon rainforest showcase a profound relationship between indigenous cultures and their environments. Through the worship of Pachamama and the shamanistic use of ayahuasca, these communities maintain a balance with nature that is vital not only for their survival but for the health of our planet. Understanding and respecting these traditions are crucial as they offer insights into sustainable living and the deep spiritual wealth of indigenous cultures.

Resurgence of the Ancient Ways

Modern Paganism, or Neo-Paganism, encompasses a diverse collection of contemporary religious movements that seek to revive and reinterpret pre-Christian, indigenous, and polytheistic traditions for the modern era. These movements, including Wicca, Druidry, and Heathenry, have gained significant momentum in the 20th and 21st centuries. Characterized by their reverence for nature, belief in multiple deities, and the practice of ritual magic, these traditions offer an alternative to the monotheistic and secular paradigms that dominate much of Western spirituality. This article explores the revival of these ancient practices, their core beliefs, and their adaptation to the contemporary world.

Historical Revival and Philosophical Foundations

The modern Pagan movement began to coalesce in the mid-20th century, particularly in Britain and the United States. It was partly inspired by romanticist and occult movements of the 19th century, which idealized the pre-Christian beliefs of Europe and emphasized a deep connection with the natural world. Wicca, one of the most prominent forms of modern Paganism, was introduced in the 1950s by Gerald Gardner, a retired British civil servant and amateur anthropologist, who claimed it to be a survival of ancient European witchcraft traditions.

Like Wicca, other Neo-Pagan paths such as Druidry and Heathenry have sought to revive and adapt the pre-Christian traditions of Celtic and Norse peoples respectively. These movements are not mere historical reenactments but are dynamic spiritual paths that integrate ancient wisdom with contemporary concerns. Central to these traditions is a polytheistic worldview, with deities and spirits honored as distinct entities that interact with the world and its inhabitants.

Beliefs in Polytheism, Nature Worship, and Magic

Polytheism is a hallmark of Neo-Pagan spirituality, with practices that honor multiple gods and goddesses, each embodying different aspects of life and nature. These deities are often seen as representations of natural forces and human archetypes, whose qualities and stories offer insights into the human condition and the workings of the cosmos. For instance, in Wicca, the Goddess and the God are revered as central deities representing nature's feminine and masculine forces.

Nature worship is another critical aspect, with rituals and festivals that follow the cycles of the seasons and lunar phases. Celebrations such as the solstices, equinoxes, and moon phases are significant, as they symbolize the ever-turning wheel of the year and the intimate connection between human life and the natural environment. These practices emphasize sustainability and ecological awareness, reflecting a worldview that respects and cherishes the Earth as a living, sacred entity.

The practice of magic—defined in Neo-Paganism as the art of causing change to occur in accordance with will—is also integral to these spiritual paths. Rituals often involve casting spells, performing enchantments, and crafting amulets, which are seen as ways to harness natural energies to influence personal, communal, or environmental situations. This magical practice is not considered supernatural but rather as part of the natural interaction between humans and the divine cosmos.

Modern Context and Community Impact

In adapting ancient practices to modern contexts, Neo-Pagan communities strongly emphasise personal experience and autonomy in spiritual matters. There is a distinctive ethos of tolerance and inclusivity, with a flexible doctrinal structure that allows practitioners to tailor their paths to personal spiritual needs. As a result, Neo-Paganism has developed a culture of intense personal spiritual development, feminist theology, and social activism.

The rise of the Internet and social media has also played a crucial role in the spread and organization of Neo-Pagan communities. Online platforms allow practitioners worldwide to share resources, discuss philosophical and theological matters, and coordinate events, helping sustain a globally connected community that is continually evolving.

The resurgence of ancient spiritual practices through modern Paganism represents a significant cultural and religious development in the contemporary world. By reviving and reinterpreting old traditions, Neo-Pagan movements challenge the dominant spiritual narratives and offer a deeply personal and ecologically integrated approach to religion. As these movements grow, they continue to adapt, influencing and being influenced by the broader cultural currents of our times, and contributing to the rich diversity of global spirituality.

Preserving Spirituality Amidst Modern Challenges

Indigenous and Pagan communities face many challenges in the modern era, from the erosion of cultural identities to conflicts over land rights and the commercialization of their spiritual practices. These challenges are not only a threat to their spiritual and cultural heritage but also to the social and ecological wisdom these traditions uphold. This article explores the contemporary issues confronting these communities, the efforts underway to preserve their traditions, and the significant role these practices play in contemporary social and environmental justice movements.

One of the most pressing issues for many indigenous communities is the erosion of their culture, which is often tightly interwoven with their spiritual practices. This erosion is exacerbated by the dwindling number of fluent speakers of indigenous languages, as younger generations become increasingly assimilated into dominant cultures. The loss of language is critical as it carries nuanced knowledge and practices that are not easily translated, thus leading to a loss of cultural depth and connection to ancestral wisdom.

Land Rights Conflicts

Land is not merely a physical space for indigenous and Pagan communities; it is a living entity, imbued with spiritual significance and ancestral presence. However, many of these communities face ongoing battles to retain rights to their ancestral lands. These conflicts often arise from governmental and corporate interests in exploiting land for resources without the consent of its indigenous inhabitants. Such disputes threaten the physical well-being of these communities and their spiritual practices and autonomy.

Commercialization of Spiritual Practices

The commercialization of indigenous and Pagan spiritual practices poses another significant challenge. Elements of these traditions are often appropriated and sold by those outside the community, stripped of their original meaning and used for profit. This commercialization not only disrespects and dilutes the sacredness of the practices but also deprives the communities of control over their own spiritual heritage.

Efforts to Preserve Traditions

In response to these challenges, numerous initiatives have been undertaken to preserve and revitalize indigenous and Pagan traditions. These include community-based education programs aimed at teaching younger generations their ancestral languages and practices and using modern technologies to record and disseminate traditional knowledge. Legal battles have also been fought to secure land rights and prevent the unauthorized use of indigenous cultural and spiritual symbols.

Furthermore, there has been a growing movement within these communities to establish and enforce guidelines around the ethical sharing of their spiritual practices to combat cultural appropriation and ensure that those participating in or facilitating such practices do so with respect and proper understanding.

Role in Social and Environmental Justice Movements

Indigenous and Pagan communities often strongly emphasise living in harmony with the environment, which positions them uniquely in the global movements for environmental justice. Their spiritual practices frequently include principles of sustainability that contrast sharply with the exploitative practices of modern industrial society. As such, these communities are increasingly recognized as vital voices in environmental dialogues, where their deep-seated knowledge and respect for the natural world can guide efforts towards sustainability.

Moreover, the spiritual framework of many indigenous and Pagan traditions, which stresses the interconnectedness of life and the importance of community and solidarity, also lends strength to social justice movements. These movements seek to address economic and social inequalities and reshape how societies understand their relationship with the earth and each other.

The challenges faced by indigenous and Pagan communities are daunting yet met with resilience and creativity. As they navigate the complexities of preserving their traditions in a rapidly changing world, these communities strive to protect their heritage and offer profound insights into living more harmoniously within the natural world. Their continued existence and resistance are testament to the enduring power of their spiritual practices and their crucial role in the global conversations on cultural integrity and environmental sustainability.

Chapter 6: New Age and Hybrid Spiritual Movements

In the vast landscape of contemporary spirituality, New Age and hybrid spiritual movements represent a significant and dynamic facet. Emerging in the mid-20th century and gaining momentum through the following decades, these movements encapsulate a profound shift in spiritual consciousness, marked by a move away from orthodox religious traditions towards more eclectic, personalized spiritual experiences. This chapter delves into the colorful world of New Age spirituality and the various hybrid movements that have arisen from blending traditional and contemporary spiritual practices.

The New Age movement, with its origins deeply rooted in the countercultural ideas of the 1960s and 1970s, draws heavily on both Eastern and Western spiritual and metaphysical traditions and the burgeoning fields of psychology and science. It is characterized by an open-ended structure and a holistic worldview, emphasizing personal growth, the interconnectedness of all existence, and the potential for direct personal divine experience.

This chapter will explore how New Age spirituality has not only influenced but has been shaped by cultural, technological, and social changes. It will examine the core beliefs that unite various New Age practices, from astrology and channeling to energy healing and beyond. Additionally, it will cover how these beliefs and practices are often integrated into people's lives alongside more traditional religious practices, creating hybrid forms of spirituality that reflect the complex nature of modern belief systems.

Moreover, the discussion will extend to the commercial aspects of the New Age movement—examining how spirituality has been marketed and how this commercialization impacts the authenticity and perception of New Age practices. Critiques of the movement, including accusations of superficiality and commodification, will also be addressed to provide a balanced view.

New Age and hybrid spiritual movements are not static; they evolve with shifting cultural tides and continue to adapt to new scientific insights and societal needs. As such, this chapter will also speculate on the future of these movements, considering how they might continue to transform in response to global challenges such as environmental crisis and social inequality.

Origins and Evolution of New Age Movements

The New Age movement, with its colorful tapestry of beliefs and practices, emerged as a distinct cultural phenomenon in the mid-20th century. This movement is characterized by its eclectic nature and profound syncretism, drawing from a myriad of sources including Eastern spiritualities, modern psychotherapy, and the burgeoning human potential movement. The historical context of the 1960s and 1970s—marked by a counter-cultural revolution against the social norms and political crises of the time—provided fertile ground for the growth of New Age thought, which promised personal enlightenment and a new way of understanding the universe.

Counter-Culture and Eastern Influences

The counter-culture of the 1960s and 1970s in the United States and Europe was a powerful catalyst for the exploration of new spiritual landscapes. Disillusioned by the materialism, war, and oppression seen in mainstream society, young people began to reject the dogmatic religious structures of their parents' generation. This period saw a significant influx of Eastern spiritual teachings into the West, as figures like Maharishi Mahesh Yogi and Chögyam Trungpa introduced transcendental meditation and Tibetan Buddhism to a Western audience hungry for spiritual meaning.

Incorporating practices such as yoga, meditation, and a philosophy emphasising the interconnectedness of all life, Eastern spiritualities offered an appealing alternative to traditional Western religious doctrines, often perceived as overly institutionalized and spiritually empty. These Eastern influences not only expanded the spiritual horizons of New Age adherents but also introduced them to the concept of achieving higher states of consciousness and personal transformation through inner work.

Psychotherapy and the Human Potential Movement

Simultaneously, the fields of psychotherapy and the nascent human potential movement began exploring the depths of human consciousness, with pioneers like Carl Jung and Abraham Maslow influencing the spiritual narrative. Jung's ideas about the collective unconscious and archetypes resonated with New Age thinking, marrying the psychological with the spiritual. Maslow's theory of self-actualization proposed that the highest motivation of humans is the pursuit of personal growth and understanding, which is aligned closely with New Age practices.

Esalen Institute in California became a hub for the human potential movement, offering workshops and sessions that integrated bodywork, meditation, and group therapy—activities that became staples in New Age practices. These sessions emphasized holistic health, suggesting that true well-being comes from harmony between the mind, body, and spirit, a concept that remains a pillar of New Age philosophy.

Metaphysics and Syncretic Religious Approaches

As the New Age movement matured, it increasingly embraced a wide array of metaphysical practices and beliefs, from astrology and tarot to channeling and past-life regression. These practices reflect a worldview that the physical universe is interwoven with invisible energies and spiritual dimensions that humans can learn to access and influence.

Moreover, New Age spirituality is inherently syncretic, often cherry-picking elements from various religions and philosophies to create a personalized spiritual framework that eschews orthodox boundaries. This syncretism is evident in how New Age practitioners might draw simultaneously from Buddhism's mindfulness, Christian mysticism's contemplation, and pagan rituals' earth-centered spirituality.

The origins of the New Age movement in the transformative decades of the 1960s and 1970s have left a lasting legacy on its structure and beliefs. New Age spirituality offers a unique and flexible approach to personal and cosmic understanding by blending Eastern spiritual practices with Western psychotherapeutic techniques and rich metaphysical traditions. As we continue into the 21st century, the influence of New Age thought persists, adapting to new scientific discoveries and cultural shifts, yet always retaining its core aim of elevating human consciousness and promoting a holistic view of health and the universe.

Exploring the Core Beliefs and Practices of New Age Spirituality

New Age spirituality, with its eclectic and inclusive nature, offers a unique perspective on the universe and our place within it. Emphasizing personal growth, self-realization, and the pursuit of higher consciousness, this modern spiritual path draws upon a variety of traditions and practices to enhance spiritual wellness and personal empowerment. This article delves into the central tenets and practices that define New Age thought, illustrating how each contributes to the broader goals of holistic health and spiritual development.

At the heart of New Age philosophy is the belief in a holistic universe—an interconnected and interdependent cosmos where everything that exists resonates with everything else. This worldview posits that personal and cosmic health are inseparable, advocating for a balanced life that nurtures the body, mind, and spirit. Central to achieving this balance is the focus on personal growth and self-realization. New Age spirituality encourages individuals to explore their own potential and transcend traditional boundaries of understanding, pushing towards higher states of consciousness.

Meditation is a cornerstone practice within New Age spirituality, revered for its calming effects and ability to expand the mind and foster a deeper connection with the universe. Through various forms of meditation, practitioners aim to quiet the mind, enhance their awareness, and achieve a state of inner peace that reflects the harmony of the holistic universe. This practice supports other aspects of New Age spirituality by providing a grounded and centered state from which individuals can explore other spiritual dimensions.

Astrology in the New Age context goes beyond simple horoscopes, offering a complex and nuanced tool for understanding the influences that shape our lives and destinies. New Age astrology incorporates traditional methods but often expands them to include a more psychological and spiritual interpretation of the celestial bodies' movements. Practitioners use astrology to gain insights into their personal characteristics, life challenges, and spiritual destinies, viewing the alignment of planets as a map to personal and spiritual development.

Channeling, another practice embraced within New Age circles, involves communicating with spiritual entities or higher consciousness forms, including angels, spirit guides, or even interdimensional beings. This practice is intended to bring forth wisdom, peace, and guidance from the spiritual world, helping individuals to make enlightened decisions and grow spiritually. Channelers often serve as mediums, delivering messages that are believed to contain universal truths and deep insights into the nature of existence.

Energy healing, including practices such as Reiki, operates on the premise that the body is surrounded by an energy field that can affect one's health and well-being. Reiki practitioners use their hands to channel energy to another person to enhance healing and restore balance within the body's energy systems. Similarly, crystal healing utilizes the natural energies of crystals and gemstones to align, heal, and transform the body's energy centers or chakras.

Both practices reflect the New Age belief in the interconnectivity of all things and the ability to influence one's physical and spiritual health through energetic means. They are often sought for stress relief, emotional healing, and as support for physical ailments, showcasing the New Age commitment to healing the whole person.

The practices and beliefs of New Age spirituality form a comprehensive approach aimed at enhancing individual awareness and deepening spiritual connections. Whether through meditation, astrology, channeling, or energy work, the goal remains consistent: to foster an alignment with the holistic universe and empower personal and spiritual growth. As we continue to navigate modern life's complexities, New Age spirituality's principles offer pathways not just to personal fulfillment but to a deeper understanding of the cosmic interplay at the heart of existence.

Technology's Role in Shaping New Age Spirituality

In the modern era, technology, particularly the internet and social media, has played a pivotal role in reshaping spiritual practices, including those within New Age movements. These digital platforms have facilitated the widespread dissemination of spiritual knowledge and fostered the creation of vibrant online communities and even the development of digital rituals. This article explores how these technological advancements have made New Age practices more accessible, customizable, and integrated into daily life, significantly altering the landscape of modern spirituality.

The Spread of Spiritual Knowledge through Digital Channels

The advent of the internet has democratized access to information, including the vast and varied teachings of New Age spirituality. Before the digital era, those interested in esoteric knowledge often had to seek out niche bookstores or specific spiritual retreats. Now, a vast repository of information is available at the click of a button. Websites, online libraries, and e-books have made spiritual texts and teachings accessible globally, removing geographical and economic barriers to knowledge.

Moreover, the internet has enabled the proliferation of multimedia resources like podcasts, webinars, and YouTube channels dedicated to topics ranging from astrology and metaphysics to crystal healing and energy work. These resources cater to a range of engagement levels, from the casually curious to the deeply devout, allowing individuals to tailor their exposure and involvement according to personal preference.

Creation and Cultivation of Online Spiritual Communities

Social media platforms have been instrumental in gathering like-minded individuals into cohesive communities that might not otherwise have the means to connect. These digital communities provide spaces for individuals to share experiences, insights, and practices, thereby enriching each other's spiritual journeys. More importantly, they offer a sense of belonging and support, which are crucial for personal growth and spiritual development.

Facebook groups, Reddit forums, and specialized apps for spirituality serve as gathering points for discussions and exchange of ideas. They also facilitate the organization of events, both virtual and physical, thereby fostering a hybrid spiritual practice that spans online and offline realms.

Emergence of Digital Rituals

Perhaps one of the most intriguing developments in New Age spirituality facilitated by technology is the emergence of digital rituals. These rituals adapt traditional practices into formats suitable for virtual participation, which has been particularly significant during periods when gathering in person has been restricted, such as during the COVID-19 pandemic.

Virtual meditation sessions, online full moon ceremonies, and streamed healing sessions have become commonplace. These digital rituals allow participants to engage in real-time with facilitators and other participants, thus extending the communal and interactive aspects of New Age practices beyond physical boundaries. They also allow for a personalization of the experience, as participants can often interact with these rituals from the comfort of their own sacred spaces at home.

Customization and Personalization of Practices

The digital era has ushered in unprecedented levels of customization and personalization in spirituality. Algorithms and data analytics allow for tailored spiritual content that matches individual interests and developmental stages. Mobile apps offer personalized astrology readings, meditation guidance based on mood or need, and even tarot readings with interpretations.

This level of customization enhances individual engagement with New Age practices and makes these traditions more adaptable to the diverse needs and rhythms of modern life. Individuals can integrate spirituality seamlessly into their daily routines, making practices like meditation and mindfulness accessible amid the demands of contemporary living.

Technology has profoundly influenced the practice and proliferation of New Age spirituality, breaking down barriers and fostering innovations that have enriched spiritual practices. As technology evolves, it will undoubtedly change how spiritual knowledge is disseminated and how communities engage with the sacred. This symbiosis between spirituality and technology reflects the dynamic nature of New Age movements and their capacity to adapt and thrive in the modern world.

The Rise of Hybrid Spiritual Movements

Spirituality has undergone significant transformations in an era characterized by its unprecedented connectivity and cultural exchange. One of the most fascinating developments in contemporary religious practice is the emergence of hybrid spiritual movements. These movements represent a blending of traditional religious elements with practices from New Age spirituality and other diverse spiritual traditions. This fusion reflects a global society increasingly inclined towards spiritual inclusivity and innovation, where boundaries between distinct religious identities become permeable. This article explores the formation of these hybrid spiritual movements, examining how they integrate elements from various traditions to create rich, multifaceted spiritual experiences.

Christian Mysticism and Eastern Meditation

A prominent example of a hybrid spiritual movement is the integration of Christian mysticism with meditation techniques derived from Eastern traditions such as Buddhism and Hinduism. This synthesis is seen in practices where Christian prayer and contemplation merge with mindfulness and meditation techniques to deepen the spiritual experience and enhance the practitioner's connection to the divine.

Institutions like the World Community for Christian Meditation have been instrumental in promoting this blend, advocating meditation as a form of prayer that deepens the faith experience without diluting Christian doctrine. This approach enriches individual spirituality and offers a fresh perspective on ancient Christian practices, making them more accessible and relevant to contemporary seekers.

Shamanic Practices and Western Psychotherapy

Another significant example of hybrid spirituality involves the integration of shamanic practices from indigenous cultures with methods derived from Western psychotherapy. This combination recognizes the therapeutic potential of shamanic rituals, particularly in dealing with psychological and emotional healing.

Practitioners of this hybrid approach use techniques such as drumming, journeying, and nature retreats, often alongside more conventional therapeutic practices like talk therapy and cognitive-behavioral techniques. The result is a holistic treatment method that addresses mental health issues from both spiritual and psychological perspectives. Programs such as those offered by the Foundation for Shamanic Studies demonstrate how these integrated practices can be used effectively to promote healing and personal growth.

Yoga and Christian Spirituality

Integrating yoga—a practice rooted in Hindu philosophy—with Christian spirituality is another example of a hybrid spiritual movement. In this melding, yoga is not only approached as a physical exercise but as a spiritual practice that can enhance prayer and meditation in a Christian context. This adaptation, sometimes called "Holy Yoga," uses biblical scriptures as mantras and frames yoga postures as a form of worship and a way to enhance one's connection to God.

Despite some controversy from purists in both camps, this hybrid practice has grown in popularity, indicating a strong desire among modern spiritual seekers to explore new forms of spiritual expression that resonate more deeply with their personal beliefs and experiences.

The Role of Technology in Facilitating Hybrid Movements

The rise of hybrid spiritual movements has been significantly facilitated by technology, particularly the internet. Online platforms allow for sharing ideas and practices across geographic and cultural boundaries, enabling an unprecedented synthesis of spiritual traditions. Websites, online workshops, and virtual retreats provide access to a wide array of teachings and practices, allowing individuals to tailor their spiritual journey to their unique needs and interests.

Hybrid spiritual movements represent a natural evolution in the world's religious landscape, driven by an increasing global consciousness and a collective desire for deeper spiritual authenticity. Drawing from a diverse array of spiritual traditions, these movements provide richer spiritual experiences and foster a greater understanding and respect among different faith communities. As society continues to evolve, these hybrid practices will likely play a crucial role in shaping the future of spirituality, highlighting the continuous human quest for connection and transcendence in an ever-changing world.

Elena Ray

New Age Movements and Environmentalism

In the diverse tapestry of contemporary spirituality, New Age movements have emerged as significant proponents of environmentalism, intertwining spiritual practices with activism to advocate for a more harmonious relationship with nature. This alignment is not merely incidental but is deeply embedded in New Age philosophy, which sees the earth as a living entity whose health is intimately connected to the well-being of humanity. This article explores how New Age beliefs and practices emphasize the interconnection of all life and how this worldview has inspired environmental activism and influenced broader ecological movements.

The Philosophical Roots of New Age Environmentalism

At the core of New Age thought is a profound recognition of the unity and interconnectedness of all existence. Both ancient spiritual traditions and contemporary understandings of the universe heavily influence this perspective. In this view, the earth is not merely a resource to be exploited, but a sacred mother, a living organism of which humans are a part, not apart. This holistic view fosters a sense of deep reverence for the natural world and a responsibility to protect and nurture the environment.

Practices that Promote Ecological Harmony

Many practices associated with the New Age movement reflect this ecological sensibility. For instance, rituals and ceremonies often incorporate elements of nature, such as water, stones, and plants, which are used with a spirit of gratitude and respect. Moreover, practices such as meditation are frequently taught as ways of attuning oneself to the earth's natural rhythms, enhancing personal well-being in alignment with environmental health.

Herbalism and natural medicine, also prevalent in New Age communities, promote the use of organic and locally sourced materials, supporting sustainable practices and reducing environmental harm. Similarly, the New Age emphasis on dietary choices that promote health—such as vegetarianism and veganism—is often linked to concerns about the environmental impact of meat production and the ethical treatment of animals.

Activism and Advocacy in New Age Environmentalism

Beyond individual practices, the ecological ethos of New Age spirituality has translated into active involvement in environmental advocacy. New Age groups are often at the forefront of environmental campaigns, advocating for policies that protect natural habitats, conserve resources, and reduce pollution. These activities are seen not just as political engagement, but as an extension of spiritual practice—a concrete application of their holistic beliefs.

The New Age movement has also contributed to the rise of the "ecospirituality" movement, which explicitly connects spiritual practice with ecological activism. Ecospirituality goes beyond traditional conservation efforts to include spiritual elements that emphasize a sacred connection to the earth and the inherent value of all forms of life.

Influence on Broader Environmental Movements

The influence of New Age thinking on broader environmental movements can be seen in the growing popularity of concepts such as Gaia theory, which posits that the earth functions as a single organism. Many environmentalists have embraced this theory as a framework for understanding the global impact of human activities on diverse ecosystems. Moreover, the New Age focus on global consciousness has helped shape the global warming and climate change narrative, framing these issues in terms of planetary health and spiritual crisis.

New Age movements have carved a unique niche within the environmental movement by infusing ecological activism with spiritual significance. This approach not only enriches the environmental movement with a deeper moral and ethical dimension but also broadens the appeal of activism by connecting it to personal spiritual growth and global consciousness. As the planet faces increasing ecological challenges, the integration of spirituality and environmentalism offered by New Age movements provides a holistic way forward, suggesting that the healing of the earth can go hand in hand with the spiritual development of humanity.

The Cultural and Future Impact of New Age and Hybrid Spiritual Movements

In the contemporary cultural landscape, New Age and hybrid spiritual movements have exerted a significant influence, permeating various aspects of mainstream culture from music and literature to popular media. These movements, characterized by their eclectic spirituality and openness to syncretic practices, have changed how spirituality is perceived and practiced and shaped cultural expressions and societal norms. This article explores the broad cultural impacts of these movements and contemplates their future trajectory in light of global spiritual trends and societal transformations.

Cultural Penetration and Influence

The cultural impact of New Age and hybrid spiritual movements is most visibly manifested in   music and the arts. The 1960s and 1970s, pivotal decades for the rise of these movements, saw artists and musicians embedding New Age themes into their work. Bands like The Beatles ventured into Indian classical music and transcendental meditation, introducing Western audiences to these elements through their massively popular platforms. This integration helped popularize and normalize diverse spiritual practices through mainstream music.

In literature, New Age themes have been explored by authors who intertwine spirituality with narrative storytelling. Books like "The Celestine Prophecy" by James Redfield and "The Alchemist" by Paulo Coelho achieved bestseller status and sparked discussions on spirituality and personal destiny, reflecting a growing public interest in themes of mysticism and self-discovery. These works, and others like them, have brought New Age concepts to the fore of public consciousness, making them everyday conversation topics.

The influence extends into popular media, with films and television shows incorporating elements such as magic, mysticism, and a deep connection to nature that resonate with New Age and pagan beliefs. From the magical realism in films like "Avatar" to the introspective journeys in series like "Sense8," the media's portrayal of these themes reflects a broader cultural acceptance and curiosity about spirituality beyond traditional religious frameworks.

Impact on Social and Personal Paradigms

Beyond the arts, New Age and hybrid spiritual movements have influenced societal attitudes towards health, wellness, and the environment. The holistic health movement, which emphasizes body, mind, and spirit interconnectedness, owes much to New Age thought. Practices like yoga, meditation, and alternative medicine, once considered fringe, have now been widely adopted as beneficial health practices. This shift is indicative of a broader cultural trend towards integrating spiritual well-being with physical and mental health.

Moreover, the environmental movement has been profoundly shaped by the spiritual view that humans are stewards of the Earth. New Age thinking often propagates this perspective, which advocates for living in harmony with the environment and emphasizes the spiritual repercussions of ecological actions. This has encouraged a shift in how environmentalism is approached, framing it not just as a scientific or economic issue but as a deeply spiritual one.

Future Directions and Global Trends

Looking ahead, the trajectory of New Age and hybrid spiritual movements appears to be intertwined with global spiritual trends and societal changes. As the world becomes more interconnected, the exchange of spiritual ideas and practices is likely to increase, potentially leading to more hybrid forms of spirituality. These movements are well-positioned to adapt to this changing spiritual landscape due to their inherent flexibility and openness to diverse beliefs and practices.

Furthermore, as societal challenges grow, particularly in terms of environmental crises and global health issues, the principles of New Age and hybrid spirituality—such as interconnectedness, sustainability, and holistic wellness—may play a crucial role in shaping responses to these challenges. These movements could drive a deeper societal shift towards sustainability and ethical living, guided by spiritual principles.

The cultural impact of New Age and hybrid spiritual movements is profound and far-reaching, influencing the arts, societal norms, and personal lifestyles. As these movements continue to evolve, they are

Elena Ray

likely to play a significant role in shaping not just spiritual but also societal responses to future global challenges. In this way, New Age and hybrid spiritualities are not only a reflection of contemporary spiritual and cultural dynamics but also a potential guiding force for future transformations.

Part III: Practices and Rituals

Chapter 7: Spiritual Practices

Spiritual practices form the core of individual and communal religious life, offering pathways to enlightenment, solace, and deeper connection with the divine. Across the globe and throughout history, these practices have served as essential components of personal development and cultural identity. In Chapter 7, we explore the rich and varied world of spiritual practices, delving into the rituals, disciplines, and activities that diverse cultures and religions employ to cultivate spiritual awareness and growth.

This exploration spans Buddhist monks' meditative stillness, Christian worshippers' fervent prayers, the disciplined fasts of Muslim devotees, and beyond, illustrating the universal human pursuit of higher truth and inner peace. Each practice, whether it involves quiet reflection, physical abstention, or joyful celebration, is a thread in the fabric of spiritual life, woven to transcend the mundane to reach the sacred.

The practices discussed in this chapter are not merely religious obligations but are acts imbued with deep symbolic significance. They are means of communicating with the supernatural, tools for transforming consciousness, and methods for fostering community cohesion. Through meditation and mindfulness, individuals seek clarity and calmness; through prayer and devotion, they forge a personal connection with the divine; through fasting and asceticism, they exercise self-control and purification; and through pilgrimages and sacred travel, they embark on journeys that are as much about internal discovery as they are about external exploration.

Furthermore, we will look at how these practices are integrated into daily life, marking the rhythm of the spiritual and secular calendar through rituals and ceremonies that celebrate life's milestones and seasonal cycles. Sacred texts and spiritual literature provide wisdom and guidance, while art and iconography serve as focal points for devotion and meditation. Dance and movement, often overlooked, are also vital expressions of spiritual energy and community harmony.

In examining these practices, we gain insight into the specific traditions of different faiths and uncover the shared human aspirations that these practices reveal. Spirituality, in its many forms, reflects humanity's enduring quest to understand the cosmos and our place within it, to cope with the existential dilemmas of life and death, and to live in harmony with the world around us. As we navigate the various spiritual practices detailed in this chapter, we invite readers to appreciate the depth and diversity of the human spiritual experience and consider how these ancient practices might hold relevance in our modern lives.

Meditation and Mindfulness

In today's fast-paced world, the ancient practices of meditation and mindfulness have gained renewed relevance, transcending cultural and religious boundaries to offer solace and clarity to millions. Rooted deeply in spiritual traditions but also embraced in non-religious contexts, these practices are celebrated for their profound impact on personal well-being and spiritual growth. This article explores the various forms of meditation and mindfulness, delves into their historical origins, and examines their benefits in fostering a deeper connection with oneself and the broader universe.

Meditation, as a formal practice, is most commonly associated with the spiritual traditions of Asia, particularly within Buddhism and Hinduism. In Buddhism, meditation is an essential part of the Eightfold Path to enlightenment, typified by practices like Vipassana (insight meditation) and Zen meditation, which focus on cultivating deep awareness and tranquility. Hinduism introduces meditation through the Yoga Sutras of Patanjali, where it serves as a crucial step towards achieving 'moksha', or liberation.

Interestingly, contemplative practices can also be found in the Christian tradition, where they take the form of prayerful reflection and contemplation, aiming to foster a closer relationship with the divine. Similar meditative practices can be observed in Islamic Sufism, which includes techniques such as dhikr, the repetitive chanting of the names of God to deepen faith and consciousness.

In contemporary settings, meditation and mindfulness have been adapted for secular purposes, greatly influenced by their proven benefits in stress reduction and mental health. The development of programs like Mindfulness-Based Stress Reduction (MBSR) has introduced these practices to a broader audience, emphasizing their role in enhancing mental and physical health independent of any religious context. These adaptations are supported by a growing body of scientific research that underscores meditation's positive effects on various aspects of neurological health, such as enhancing concentration, reducing symptoms of anxiety and depression, and even potentially slowing aging.

Forms and Techniques

Meditation and mindfulness manifest in various forms, each with its unique focus and techniques. For instance:

> **Mindfulness Meditation**: Encourages acute awareness of the present moment, typically focusing on breath or bodily sensations. Practitioners learn to observe thoughts and feelings without judgment, fostering a state of calm awareness.

> **Transcendental Meditation**: Involves chanting a mantra during meditation to achieve deeper states of relaxation and spiritual growth.

> **Guided Meditation**: Uses verbal instruction either in person or via a recording to guide one's thoughts toward a relaxed and focused state, often using visualizations.

Each style of meditation offers different pathways to the same goal: greater peace, clarity, and self-awareness, proving that this ancient practice can be tailored to meet the diverse needs of individuals today.

Benefits of Meditation and Mindfulness

The benefits of engaging in regular meditation and mindfulness are extensive. Psychologically, they help reduce stress, anxiety, and depression. Physiologically, they have been found to lower blood pressure, improve immune function, and aid sleep. Spiritually, these practices provide a pathway to greater personal and existential awareness, helping individuals understand their place in the world and connect more deeply with whatever they consider divine.

Integration into Daily Life

Today, meditation and mindfulness are not just practices reserved for retreats or spiritual communities but integrated into daily life. Many find that even a few minutes of meditation each day can profoundly affect their quality of life, enhancing their overall well-being and ability to cope with the challenges of modern living.

As meditation and mindfulness continue to spread across cultural and religious lines, their role in promoting a healthier, more conscious society becomes ever more apparent. They offer a calm refuge in the storm of modern life, providing tools to help anyone achieve greater peace and mental clarity. The continued evolution of these practices promises further integration into daily routines and healthcare systems worldwide, highlighting their universal appeal and timeless relevance.

Prayer and Devotion

Prayer is a profound facet of human spirituality, a practice as old as faith itself, found in every corner of the world and across all cultures. It is the spiritual lifeline through which individuals communicate with something greater than themselves—be it God, gods, the universe, or another form of a higher power. This article explores the various expressions of prayer—from spoken words to silent contemplation—and examines its role and significance in different religious traditions. It delves into how prayer serves not only as a practice of worship but also as a vital instrument for seeking guidance, expressing gratitude, and fostering a deep, personal connection with the divine.

Prayer manifests in numerous forms across the spiritual spectrum. In Christianity, prayer can range from formal, liturgical recitations found in Catholic Masses to Evangelical Christians' spontaneous and personal prayers. Similarly, Islam practices structured prayers like the Salat, performed five times a day facing Mecca, embodying a form of worship that is both an act of discipline and devotion.

In contrast, Hinduism offers a more visually and ritually diverse form of prayer, involving words and offerings such as flowers, food, and incense in ceremonies like Puja, which seek to honor and receive blessings from various deities. Meanwhile, in Buddhism, prayer does not assume communication with a creator god but is instead often a form of meditation, focusing on the individual's inner transformation and the cultivation of compassion and mindfulness.

Silent contemplation or meditation is another profound form of prayer found in many traditions, including Christianity's contemplative prayer, which seeks to experience God's presence by being attentive and responsive to Him in silence. This form of prayer is less about speaking to the divine and more about listening, allowing space for the inner stirrings of the soul to surface and be acknowledged.

The role of prayer in religious and spiritual life is multifaceted. At its core, prayer is an act of worship, a fundamental expression of belief. It serves as a direct line to the divine, a way for believers to strengthen their faith and seek comfort and assurance from their spiritual anchors.

Prayer is also instrumental in seeking guidance. In moments of uncertainty or decision-making, individuals turn to prayer to seek clarity from higher powers. This is often accompanied by requests for divine intervention, where prayer becomes a solace, providing hope and the possibility of miracles in challenging times.

Moreover, gratitude is a powerful theme in prayer across many faiths. Expressions of thankfulness are prevalent, whether after receiving good news, experiencing a joyful event, or recognizing the divine in everyday life. This form of prayer fosters a mindset of appreciation and humility, reminding individuals of their blessings and the grace that pervades their lives.

Perhaps most importantly, prayer is about personal connection. It offers a private, intimate space where individuals can lay bare their fears, hopes, and dreams before their divine witness. This personal aspect of prayer is what makes it deeply therapeutic; it not only nurtures the soul but also helps in managing emotional and psychological stress.

As we look across the religious landscape, the universal thread of prayer—despite its diverse manifestations—highlights a common human yearning for connection with something greater than oneself. It transcends mere ritual to touch the essence of human existence and spiritual longing. As the world becomes increasingly complex, the simplicity and refuge offered by prayer become ever more valuable. Whether through words, silence, or ritual, prayer remains a central pillar of spiritual practice, continually adapting to meet the evolving spiritual needs of humanity.

Rituals and Ceremonies

Rituals and ceremonies are the vibrant threads woven into the fabric of spiritual life across cultures and religions. Serving as pivotal anchors in the lives of communities and individuals, these practices are rich with symbolism and purpose, deeply entrenched in the traditions that define human interaction with the divine and the natural world. This article explores the various facets of rituals and ceremonies, from their roles in marking significant life events and seasonal transitions to their contributions to community cohesion and personal spiritual growth.

At their core, rituals and ceremonies serve to articulate and affirm the values and beliefs of a culture or religious community. They act as vessels for conveying the sacred narratives that shape spiritual identities and practices. Whether it's a baptism ceremony signifying spiritual rebirth in Christianity, a Hindu wedding marking the sacred union of two souls, or a Pagan celebration of the Earth's seasonal cycles, each ritual is imbued with deep symbolism that resonates with the participants' shared understandings and aspirations.

These events often utilize specific symbols—water, fire, incense, colors, and more—that have rich connotations within the particular spiritual framework. For instance, water symbolizes purification, life, and rejuvenation in many rituals, while fire often represents transformation, energy, and divine presence.

One of the most prominent roles of rituals is in marking life transitions. These rites of passage—such as birth, coming of age, marriage, and death—are universal themes, and rituals help navigate the emotional landscape of these transitions. They provide a structured way to process change, incorporating elements that offer comfort, guidance, and community support. For example, the Jewish Bar and Bat Mitzvah ceremonies celebrate the transition of children into adult responsibilities within the faith, while funeral rites across different cultures provide a structured means of mourning and celebrating the life of the deceased, aiding in communal and individual healing.

Beyond individual life events, rituals and ceremonies frequently celebrate seasonal changes and spiritual milestones that highlight humanity's connection to nature and the cosmos. Many ancient and contemporary religions observe equinoxes, solstices, and harvest cycles. These celebrations, such as the Celtic Samhain or the Japanese Hanami (cherry blossom viewing), not only honor the rhythms of nature but also serve to remind communities of the cyclical nature of life and the importance of living in harmony with the environment.

Ritually marked events play crucial roles in strengthening community bonds and fostering a sense of belonging and identity among participants. By engaging in shared practices, individuals affirm their place within the community and participate in the collective expression of their cultural or spiritual values. This communal participation also contributes to personal spiritual growth, as individuals reflect on their roles within the wider community and the universe.

Furthermore, personal rituals, such as daily prayers or meditations, help individuals maintain a personal connection with their spiritual beliefs, offering a daily structure that enhances mindfulness and spiritual discipline. These personal practices are essential for ongoing spiritual maintenance and growth, providing a moment of reflection and reconnection amid the bustle of everyday life.

Rituals and ceremonies are more than just formalities; they are profound expressions of human spirituality and cultural identity. They serve as crucial mechanisms for navigating the complexities of life, enhancing communal ties, and fostering individual spiritual journeys. As we continue to evolve spiritually and culturally, these practices adapt, integrating new meanings and forms that resonate with contemporary values while remaining rooted in ancient traditions. Thus, the ongoing relevance and adaptation of rituals and ceremonies reflect the dynamic nature of human spirituality and our enduring need to find meaning and community through shared sacred practices.

Fasting and Ascetic Practices

Across various spiritual landscapes, fasting and ascetic practices are revered as profound expressions of faith, discipline, and devotion.

These practices, which often entail abstention from food, comfort, or other physical pleasures, are not merely acts of self-denial but are imbued with deep spiritual significance. This article explores the philosophies underpinning these practices, their variations across different cultures, and the spiritual benefits they are believed to confer.

Philosophical Foundations of Ascetic Practices

The belief that physical abstention leads to spiritual abundance is at the heart of most ascetic practices. This philosophy is rooted in the idea that the material body, and its desires, often distract from spiritual growth and enlightenment. By subduing these desires, practitioners believe they can purify their bodies and minds, making them more receptive to spiritual insights and divine experiences.

In many traditions, these practices are also seen as a form of sacrifice. The act of giving something up—especially something as essential as food or comfort—is viewed as an offering to a higher power, an expression of faith and complete dependence on the divine. This sacrifice is often thought to build spiritual merit, which can lead to divine blessings or favor.

Cultural Variations in Ascetic Practices

Fasting and ascetic practices manifest differently across the world's spiritual traditions, each tailored to a community's specific theological and cultural context. In Islam, for example, fasting during the month of Ramadan is one of the Five Pillars of the faith. Muslims abstain from food, drink, and other physical needs from dawn until sunset. This fast is seen as a way to cleanse the soul, practice self-discipline, and empathize with those less fortunate.

In Christianity, particularly within its Orthodox and Catholic branches, fasting is observed during Lent, the 40 days leading up to Easter. Here, fasting involves various degrees of food restriction, intended to mimic Jesus Christ's sacrifice and withdrawal into the desert for 40 days. This practice is both a preparation for the celebration of Easter and a method of fostering spiritual reflection and repentance.

Hinduism also features various ascetic practices, with fasting being a common observance during festivals and holy days, such as Shivaratri or Ekadashi. These fasts, which can vary from partial to complete abstention from food, are believed to purify the practitioner's body and mind, aiding in the attainment of spiritual goals.

In Buddhism, particularly within the Theravada tradition, monks adhere to a strict daily schedule where food is only consumed before noon and fast until the next morning. This practice supports their lifestyle of minimalism and mindfulness, essential components of their path to enlightenment.

Intended Spiritual Benefits

The spiritual benefits of fasting and asceticism are manifold. At a fundamental level, these practices are believed to purify the practitioner, not just physically but spiritually, clearing away the impurities that cloud the mind and hinder spiritual growth. They are also seen as enhancing one's discipline and self-control, qualities that are highly prized in many spiritual traditions for their role in maintaining moral integrity and focus on spiritual goals.

Moreover, these practices often lead to heightened states of spiritual awareness and ecstasy. The physical deprivation can alter one's state of consciousness, facilitating mystical experiences, visions, or deeper understanding of divine truths. These experiences are often seen as profoundly transformative, fostering a deeper, more intimate connection with the divine and a renewed sense of spiritual purpose.

Fasting and ascetic practices represent a core aspect of spiritual discipline across diverse traditions, reflecting a universal acknowledgment of the physical and spiritual interplay. While the practices themselves vary widely, their underlying purposes resonate with a common theme: by tempering the physical, one can amplify the spiritual, achieving a purer, closer connection with the divine. As modern societies grapple with material excess and spiritual scarcity, these ancient practices offer profound lessons on the value of simplicity and sacrifice in cultivating a fulfilled and meaningful life.

Pilgrimage and Sacred Travel

Pilgrimage, an ancient practice rich in spiritual significance, involves traveling to a sacred site as a seeker of enlightenment, penance, or divine blessings. This venerable tradition transcends cultural and religious boundaries, uniquely blending physical journeying and spiritual searching. This article delves into the historical and modern contexts of pilgrimages across major religious traditions, exploring both the personal and communal dimensions of these sacred journeys and their profound impact on spiritual deepening.

The act of pilgrimage is as old as religion itself, manifesting in various forms across different cultures and faiths. In the Hindu tradition, the pilgrimage to the holy city of Varanasi is believed to offer liberation from the cycle of rebirth. Muslims undertake the Hajj to Mecca, fulfilling one of the Five Pillars of Islam, while Christians might journey to the Church of the Holy Sepulchre in Jerusalem or follow the medieval pilgrimage routes to Santiago de Compostela in Spain. Each of these journeys is deeply embedded in the religious consciousness of the faithful, rooted in centuries of tradition and spiritual practice.

In modern times, pilgrimage remains a powerful spiritual practice, though its expression may vary. Modern transportation has made sacred sites more accessible, allowing more people from around the globe to participate in these transformative experiences. Despite this accessibility, the essence of pilgrimage—a profound search for deeper understanding and connection with the divine—remains unchanged. Today's pilgrims might document their journeys on social media, sharing their spiritual insights and the challenges of their travels with a global audience. Yet, the core experience of personal transformation and renewal persists.

The act of pilgrimage uniquely blends personal and communal spiritual practices. Individually, it offers a time of introspection and prayer, an opportunity to step away from the daily demands of life and focus on personal growth and spiritual renewal. Many pilgrims report experiences of profound personal revelations, a renewed sense of purpose, or deep emotional healing during their journeys.

Communally, pilgrimages bring together individuals from diverse backgrounds, fostering a sense of unity and shared purpose. This aspect is particularly evident during large gatherings like the Kumbh Mela in India or the annual Hajj, where millions of pilgrims come together in a powerful expression of faith. These gatherings reinforce the shared beliefs and values of a faith community and promote a deeper understanding and respect for fellow travelers on the spiritual path.

The impact of pilgrimage on spiritual deepening cannot be overstated. By engaging both body and spirit, pilgrimages challenge individuals to reflect on their lives and beliefs in profound and often life-changing ways. The physical exertions of the journey, combined with the spiritual and emotional trials encountered along the way, act as catalysts for personal transformation. The act of moving towards a sacred goal allows pilgrims to symbolically journey closer to the divine, mirroring their internal spiritual progress.

Moreover, visiting a site imbued with historical and spiritual significance can provide a tangible connection to the divine that is difficult to replicate in other contexts. This connection is often marked by rituals and ceremonies performed at the pilgrimage site, which can deepen one's faith and spiritual understanding.

Pilgrimage remains a vital spiritual practice in the modern world, bridging the historical with the contemporary and the personal with the communal. As both a physical and spiritual journey, it offers unparalleled opportunities for personal growth and community building. Whether seeking enlightenment, performing penance, or searching for divine blessings, pilgrims find a profound source of spiritual renewal that resonates deeply in their lives long after their return. Thus, the enduring appeal of pilgrimage highlights the intrinsic human desire for meaningful spiritual engagement and the continuous search for deeper connections with the divine.

Use of Sacred Texts and Literature

Have you ever wondered how a piece of ancient writing still influences the daily lives of millions around the globe? Sacred texts and spiritual literature are not merely historical artifacts but living documents that continue to inspire, guide, and shape the lives of countless individuals. From the Torah scrolls read in synagogues to the Bhagavad Gita's verses chanted in temples across India, these texts offer more than religious doctrine; they provide a framework for personal morality, communal identity, and spiritual practice.

The Role of Sacred Texts in Daily Spiritual Practices

How do people integrate ancient wisdom into their modern lives? For many, sacred texts are a daily source of inspiration and guidance. In Islam, the Quran plays a crucial role in the daily lives of Muslims, with specific verses recited during the five daily prayers. The practice of reading or reciting these verses helps adherents connect with their faith at regular intervals, imbuing their day-to-day routines with a sense of divine presence.

Similarly, many Christians turn to the Bible for daily devotionals. These sessions often involve reading and meditating on specific passages, seeking to apply these teachings to contemporary issues. This daily engagement helps individuals maintain a spiritual focus amid the secular pressures of modern life. Isn't it fascinating how ancient texts can offer relevant insights into modern dilemmas?

Sacred Literature in Study and Personal Reflection

Ever caught yourself pondering the deeper meaning of life? You're not alone. Study and reflection on sacred texts are foundational to many spiritual traditions. In Judaism, the study of the Talmud and the Torah can be a lifelong endeavor. Yeshivas (Jewish educational institutions) are dedicated to the rigorous study of these texts, where students engage in lively debates and discussions, delving deep into the interpretations and practical applications of the teachings.

In Hinduism, the Vedas and Upanishads are studied by religious scholars and laypersons seeking philosophical insights. These texts are often explored in study groups and spiritual retreats, where collective interpretations and discussions can lead to profound personal revelations and spiritual growth.

Communal Worship and Sacred Texts

Have you ever felt a strong sense of community in a religious gathering? The shared recitation of sacred literature often amplifies this feeling. In communal worship settings, sacred texts serve as the focal point around which communities gather and celebrate their shared beliefs. For instance, during the Sikh service at the Gurdwara, the Guru Granth Sahib is read aloud, and its teachings are discussed among the congregation. This reinforces communal bonds and ensures that the teachings directly influence community life.

In many Christian churches, scripture readings are an integral part of the worship service, with passages chosen that align with the liturgical calendar and themes relevant to the congregation's needs. This communal engagement with sacred texts enhances individual understanding and fosters a shared spiritual journey.

The Influence of Sacred Texts on Spiritual Life

Why do these texts matter so much? The influence of sacred texts extends beyond individual and communal religious practices into the wider cultural and ethical spheres. They shape laws, influence ethical discussions, and guide social justice initiatives. For example, many civil rights leaders have drawn on biblical themes of justice and liberation to advocate for social change.

Moreover, in times of personal crisis or moral dilemma, individuals often turn to sacred texts for comfort and guidance. These texts' stories, parables, and teachings provide frameworks for understanding suffering, joy, purpose, and justice, offering solace and resolution.

Sacred texts and spiritual literature are more than just words on a page; they are vibrant, dynamic elements of spiritual life that offer continuous guidance and inspiration. Whether through daily recitation, in-depth study, or communal worship, these texts play a crucial role in shaping the spiritual landscapes of communities and individuals alike. They bridge past and present, offering timeless wisdom that helps navigate the complexities of modern life. Isn't it remarkable how these ancient texts remain relevant and continue to impact lives across the globe?

Chapter 8: Sacred Rituals and Ceremonies

Rituals and ceremonies are the heartbeat of spiritual practice, embodying the essence of faith and tradition across the globe. These profound acts serve not only as expressions of belief but as vital connectors of the individual to the collective, the human to the divine, the mundane to the sacred. This chapter dig into sacred rituals and ceremonies, exploring their depth and diversity as they occur in various cultural and religious contexts.

Throughout history, rituals and ceremonies have been pivotal in shaping spiritual experiences, providing structure and meaning to life's most significant moments. Whether it's the celebration of birth, the solemnity of death, the joy of marriage, or the introspection of initiation rites, these practices offer a way to navigate the complexities of human existence. They are acts filled with symbolism, each gesture and word steeped in ancient traditions, passed down through generations and preserved within the collective memory of communities.

But what makes these rituals and ceremonies so enduring? What purposes do they serve in the lives of individuals and societies? This chapter will explore these questions by examining how rituals are intricately woven into the fabric of spiritual life, marking the passage of time, seasons, and life cycles. We will look at how these practices foster community cohesion, reinforce social norms, and facilitate personal transformation.

Each practice carries its unique signature from the grand pilgrimage ceremonies that draw millions of adherents to the simple daily rites that offer solace and connection. We will venture into the fields, temples, churches, rivers, and mountains where these rituals are performed, uncovering the sacred interactions between people, their environment, and the metaphysical realms they reach out to.

This exploration will highlight the traditional practices that have been the cornerstone of religious observance and touch upon the new and eclectic ceremonies that have emerged in our global and interconnected world. These modern adaptations and innovations continue to shape and expand the boundaries of what we understand under the umbrella of sacred rituals and ceremonies.

The Sacred Traditions of Rites of Passage

Rites of passage are profound markers in the journey of life, universally recognized yet culturally distinct. These rituals signify the transitions that define our existence—from birth, through adolescence, into adulthood, and finally at the end of life. Each culture celebrates these transitions in unique ways, embedding deep societal values and beliefs into ceremonies that highlight the progression of an individual within their community. This exploration will delve into the rites of passage from various cultures, examining their symbolic meanings and their roles in human life.

Birth and Early Life Rituals

How do we welcome a new life into the world? Across cultures, the arrival of a newborn is often marked with rituals that signify the child's integration into the family and society. In Hindu culture, the 'Namakarana' ceremony, which is the naming ritual, takes place about ten days after birth. It involves the elders naming the newborn while whispering the chosen name in the baby's ear, a practice believed to bless the child with their identity.

Similarly, in Christianity, the sacrament of baptism is performed. This ritual involves sprinkling holy water on the infant's head while parents and godparents pledge to raise the child in the faith. This ceremony introduces the child to the Christian community and symbolizes the washing away of original sin, marking the beginning of a lifelong journey of faith.

Coming of Age Ceremonies

Remember your transition from childhood to adulthood? How was it recognized in your community? Coming of age is a significant transition celebrated with elaborate rituals worldwide. Jewish Bar and Bat Mitzvahs are prime examples. When Jewish boys turn 13 and girls turn 12, they celebrate their Bar and Bat Mitzvahs, respectively, which recognize them as adults in the eyes of the Jewish community. During the ceremony, the celebrant reads from the Torah in front of the congregation, demonstrating their maturity and their readiness to take on religious responsibilities.

For the Maasai in Kenya and Tanzania, coming of age involves both boys and girls undergoing ceremonies and rituals that include circumcision. Teachings from the elders accompany these rites, imparting crucial knowledge and skills needed to navigate adult responsibilities effectively.

Wedding Ceremonies

Have you ever attended a wedding and felt the weight of the ancestral traditions being honored? Marriage ceremonies are rich with rituals that celebrate the union of two individuals and their formal acceptance into adult society as a couple. Hindu weddings, for instance, include the 'Saptapadi' or 'Seven Steps,' where the bride and groom take seven steps around a sacred fire, each step representing a marital vow and a promise to pursue life's values together.

In contrast, Christian weddings often feature the exchange of vows and rings, which symbolize commitment and eternal love. The ceremony may vary slightly between denominations but generally includes prayers, readings from the Bible, and blessings, emphasizing the sacredness of the marital union.

End-of-Life Rites

How do we say goodbye to our loved ones? This final transition is observed solemnly across all cultures. In Buddhist traditions, the focus is on serenity and detachment, helping the dying individual and their family understand and accept the impermanence of life. Chants and prayers are offered to ease the passage of the soul from this life to the next, reflecting the cycle of rebirth.

In Christianity, the last rites, also known as the Anointing of the Sick, involve a minister anointing the person with oil, praying for them, and often administering the Eucharist or Communion. This sacrament is meant to prepare the soul for passing into the next life, providing comfort and spiritual solace to the dying and their families.

From the cradle to the grave, rites of passage serve as significant milestones in our personal and communal lives. They not only mark the transition from one life stage to another but also reinforce our cultures' shared values and beliefs. In celebrating these rites, societies reaffirm their connections to each other and their heritage, preserving traditions passed down through generations. These ceremonies help individuals understand their place in the world and define their roles within their communities, ensuring that the wisdom of the past is carried forward into the future.

The Power of Healing and Purification Rituals

In every corner of the world, diverse cultures have long held sacred the practices that purify the spirit and heal the body. These rituals, deeply embedded in the spiritual traditions of societies, serve as a bridge to restore balance and expel the negative energies that disrupt wellbeing. From the sweat lodges of Native American tribes to the ancient Hindu Panchakarma and the purification rites of Shinto in Japan, each practice offers a unique lens through which we can explore the universal quest for spiritual cleanliness and health. This article delves into these fascinating rituals, examining their significance, methodologies, and the profound impacts they have on individuals and communities.

The Native American Sweat Lodge: A Ceremony of Renewal

Have you ever felt the need for a complete reset, a way to sweat out toxins, stress, and spiritual weariness? The Native American sweat lodge ceremony, or 'Inipi', might be one of the most intense purification rituals known. Traditionally used by many tribes across North America, the sweat lodge is a dome-shaped structure made from natural materials, where participants enter to experience both physical and spiritual cleansing.

Inside the lodge, stones are heated in a fire and then placed in a pit within the center of the small, enclosed space. Water is poured over these stones to create steam, which envelops the participants in intense heat. This process is accompanied by prayers, chants, and sometimes the use of sacred herbs like sage or sweetgrass, believed to enhance the cleansing process. But what happens inside a sweat lodge goes beyond mere physical detoxification; it is a deeply spiritual experience where individuals seek healing, guidance, and renewal from the spiritual forces they hold sacred.

Panchakarma: The Five Actions of Purification

Imagine a system of healing that doesn't just treat symptoms but seeks to completely renew your body and spirit. In Ayurveda, India's ancient medical system, Panchakarma is that comprehensive approach to health. Translating to 'five actions', Panchakarma is a series of procedures designed to cleanse the body of toxins and restore its constitutional balance.

This ritualistic practice involves several stages, which may include oil baths, controlled vomiting, nasal administrations, enemas, and bloodletting. Each procedure is tailored to the individual's specific health needs and constitutional type, determined by a qualified practitioner. Panchakarma is not merely about physical cleansing but is also considered a spiritual rebirth; many who undergo these rituals report profound emotional releases and awakening, illustrating the deep connection between physical health and spiritual wellbeing.

Misogi: The Shinto Practice of Purification

Have you ever stood under a waterfall, letting the water crash over you and felt somehow transformed? In Shinto, the indigenous spirituality of Japan, Misogi is a purification ritual that involves standing under a waterfall or engaging in other cleansing practices involving water. This ritual is thought to cleanse the practitioner of pollutants and impurities, both physical and spiritual.

Participants often perform Misogi in conjunction with prayers and chants, sometimes at sacred shrines or in natural settings that are believed to be imbued with spiritual significance. The cold shock and the physical challenge of the water are said to strip away impurities and revitalize the spirit, reinforcing the practitioner's mental and physical fortitude.

The Universal Appeal of Purification Rituals

Across these diverse cultures, the rituals share a common theme: the belief in the necessity of clearing out the old to make way for the new. This concept resonates with the personal experiences of many who seek out these rituals. Who among us hasn't felt the need to shed burdens and start afresh? These ceremonies provide not just a method but a sacred space for such transformations to occur.

The enduring nature of these practices—despite the advent of modern medicine and the global mixing of cultures—speaks to their fundamental efficacy and deep significance. As we continue to navigate the complexities of modern life, the ancient wisdom encapsulated in healing and purification rituals remains as relevant as ever. They offer a time-tested route to restoring balance and health, reminding us that sometimes, the best way to move forward is to cleanse and begin anew. Whether through the steam of a sweat lodge, the meticulous processes of Panchakarma, or the bracing chill of a Misogi waterfall, these rituals provide pathways to a spiritually and physically rejuvenated existence.

Seasonal and Agricultural Ceremonies

Ever paused to wonder how the changing seasons shape our spiritual and communal lives? Across the globe, agricultural societies have long celebrated the cyclical patterns of nature through a variety of rich and diverse ceremonies. Deeply ingrained in cultural traditions, these rituals are not just social events but profound expressions of gratitude and dependency on the natural world. From the Pagan Wheel of the Year to the East Asian Moon Festival and the Jewish festival of Sukkot, each ceremony is a vibrant testament to humanity's relationship with the earth and its cycles.

The Pagan Wheel of the Year: Celebrating Solstices and Equinoxes

The Pagan Wheel of the Year is a colorful illustration of how ancient traditions mark time through the natural cycles. Comprising eight festivals, including the solstices, equinoxes, and four midpoint seasons, this wheel symbolizes the endless cycle of seasonal change and agricultural rhythms. But what's the significance behind these observances?

Take, for example, Samhain, celebrated as the Pagan new year, which marks the end of the harvest and the beginning of winter. It is believed that on this night, the veil between the living and the dead is thinnest, allowing for communication with the ancestors. Isn't it fascinating how this belief in the spiritual importance of seasonal transition can alter perceptions of time and existence?

Spring Equinox, or Ostara, celebrates the renewal of life with symbols now synonymous with modern Easter: eggs and rabbits, representing fertility and new beginnings. Through these celebrations, Pagans express gratitude for the Earth's bounty and acknowledge the delicate balance of the seasons that is crucial for sustaining life.

The East Asian Moon Festival: A Time of Togetherness

Falling on the 15th day of the eighth lunar month, the Moon Festival, or Mid-Autumn Festival, is a cherished celebration across East Asia, especially in China and Vietnam. This festival celebrates the harvest during the brightest moon of the year, a symbol of abundance, prosperity, and family reunion.

Traditionally, families gather to admire the full moon, a practice believed to bring good luck and happiness. Mooncakes, rich pastries filled with sweet bean paste or lotus seed paste, are shared among family members, symbolizing completeness and unity. How powerful can a simple act of sharing food under the moonlight reinforce familial bonds and communal spirit?

Sukkot: The Jewish Harvest Festival

Sukkot, also known as the Feast of Tabernacles, is a joyous Jewish festival that occurs in autumn, following the solemn reflection of the High Holy Days. It commemorates the forty years of Jewish wandering in the desert after the Exodus from Egypt, and celebrates the harvest gathering.

During Sukkot, it is customary to construct a Sukkah, an outdoor hut covered with natural materials, where families eat, sleep, and welcome guests for seven days. This practice not only recalls the temporary shelters Israelites inhabited during their desert wanderings but also reinforces the dependence on God's protection and harvest bounty. How profound is the reminder that stability often comes from faith and community, rather than just physical structures?

As we traverse from the Pagan rituals of the ancient Celts to the communal harvest festivals of East Asia and the desert huts of Jewish tradition, it becomes clear how deeply human lives are intertwined with the rhythms of nature. These seasonal and agricultural ceremonies do more than just mark time; they are vital expressions of human gratitude, dependence, and celebration of the natural cycles that sustain us. They remind us that, despite our modern lives, we are still fundamentally connected to the earth and its seasons, dependent on its cycles for our sustenance and survival. In every grain of harvested wheat, every mooncake shared, and every sukkah built, there is a story of humanity, a dance with nature that continues to shape our spiritual landscapes.

Death and Ancestral Worship Rituals

Why do we honor the dead? Across cultures and epochs, humanity has developed rich and varied rituals to deal with death, mourn the departed, and celebrate the lives of ancestors. These practices, deeply embedded in each society's fabric, not only help the living cope with loss but also ensure that the legacies of the deceased continue to influence the community. From the vibrant altars of Mexico's Day of the Dead to the solemn offerings of China's Qingming Festival and the intricate mummification processes of ancient Egypt, each ritual provides a window into a culture's values, beliefs, and emotional landscapes.

Honoring the Dead: The Mexican Day of the Dead

Imagine streets lined with marigolds, homes adorned with vibrant altars, and families gathering in cemeteries with food, music, and tales of the departed. The Mexican Day of the Dead, or Día de los Muertos, is a powerful example of how a culture can embrace death with both joy and reverence. Occurring on November 1st and 2nd, this festival roots back to both indigenous Aztec rituals and Catholic influences. The altars, or ofrendas, are not just memorials but are believed to welcome the spirits back to the world of the living for a brief visit, filled with the pleasures they enjoyed in life. Have you ever considered what items you would place on such an altar for your loved ones?

Veneration of Ancestors: The Chinese Qingming Festival

On the other side of the world, during the Qingming Festival, also known as Tomb-Sweeping Day, Chinese families visit their ancestors' graves to clean the site, offer food, tea, and paper replicas, and burn incense. This ritual, held in early April, combines respect for the dead with the enjoyment of the arrival of spring. The practice of making offerings is meant to provide for the ancestors in the afterlife, ensuring their well-being and seeking their blessings for the family. The rituals associated with Qingming are not just about maintenance of the graves but are acts of filial piety—a core value in Confucianism.

Preserving Legacy: Ancient Egyptian Embalming and Burial

Turning to the sands of time in ancient Egypt, the embalming and burial processes were part of a complex ritual to guarantee the deceased's safe passage to the afterlife. The Egyptians believed that preserving the body through mummification was essential for the ba (soul) to recognize and return to it in the afterlife. Rich in symbolism, the rituals performed by priests involved prayers and offerings to the gods, particularly Osiris, the god of the afterlife. These practices highlight how the Egyptians viewed death as merely a transition, not an end, with the potential for eternal life.

What does this tell us about the human experience? Despite the vast differences in practices and beliefs, the rituals surrounding death and ancestral worship share common goals: to honor the dead, assist them in their spiritual journey beyond this life, and keep their memory alive within the community. These practices offer comfort to the bereaved and foster a sense of continuity between the past, present, and future. They remind us that our relationships with loved ones do not end with death but transform into a new, spiritual form of connection. As we continue to explore these sacred rituals, we gain a deeper understanding of other cultures and insights into the universal aspects of human nature and our approaches to life's ultimate transition.

Initiation and Esoteric Rituals

Why do secret societies and closed groups fascinate us so deeply? Perhaps it's the allure of hidden knowledge or the promise of deeper spiritual connections that these groups offer through their secretive initiation rituals. From the Sufi Whirling Dervishes and the Freemasons to the mystical traditions of Kabbalah, initiation and esoteric rituals are cornerstones for deepening members' spiritual paths and bonding them uniquely to their communities. This article explores these enigmatic practices, delving into their purposes, the secretive nature surrounding them, and their profound impact on those who undergo them.

The Whirling Path to Enlightenment: Sufi Dervishes

Have you ever watched in awe as Sufi dervishes spin continuously, their white robes billowing in serene circles? This dance, known as the Sema ceremony, is an artistic expression and a profound religious ritual of the Mevlevi Order in Sufism, symbolizing a mystical journey of spiritual ascent through mind and love to "Perfect." The ceremony includes several stages of symbolic meaning, including recognition of God's power, demonstrating absolute submission, and culminating in a trance state that represents the true union with the divine. The ritual serves as an initiation for the dervishes, marking their spiritual birth and commitment to the path of Sufism.

Masonic Rites of Passage: The Craft of Spiritual Architecture

Turning to the secretive halls of Freemasonry, initiation rituals are integral to this fraternal organization's structure, each designed to teach moral and philosophical lessons. These ceremonies are highly symbolic, involving elements like the checkered floor (representing good and evil within life), the compass and the square (symbolizing one's boundaries within humanity), and the All-Seeing Eye (divine observation). The initiates progress through degrees, each with its own ritual meant to impart deeper knowledge and commitment to the principles of Freemasonry, such as brotherly love, relief, and truth. Ever wondered what it truly means to be a Freemason? It's about secret handshakes and building one's moral and spiritual character.

The Kabbalistic Journey: Mystical Initiations

In the mystical tradition of Kabbalah, initiation rituals are less about ceremony and more about profound spiritual understanding and the receiving of esoteric knowledge. These rituals are typically reserved for those who have already achieved a certain level of spiritual maturity and are prepared to delve deeper into the mysteries of the universe as described in the Zohar and other sacred texts. The initiation often involves the study of complex symbols, numerology, and the Tree of Life, which maps the relationship between divine creation and the recipient's spiritual pathway. Such studies are not merely academic; they are transformative processes that change how practitioners perceive the universe and their place within it.

What can we learn from these initiation and esoteric rituals that remain shrouded in secrecy and mystique? At their core, these practices are about transformation—they are designed to challenge, enlighten, and elevate participants, offering them not just knowledge but a new way of seeing the world. Through these rituals, initiates are bonded to their fellow members and to the spiritual lineage of their tradition, equipped with tools to navigate the material and spiritual realms more profoundly. Whether through the ecstatic spins of the Whirling Dervishes, the structured rites of the Freemasons, or the mystical studies of Kabbalah, these rituals remind us of the human quest for understanding and connection, pushing us to consider how deep the journey into our own spiritual landscape might go.

Eclectic and Modern Rituals

How are spiritual practices evolving in an era of rapid change and cultural fusion? The development of new rituals and ceremonies in modern spiritual landscapes, particularly within New Age movements and interfaith groups, offers a fascinating glimpse into the dynamic nature of contemporary spirituality. These innovative practices reflect a shift towards inclusivity and personal expression, drawing on diverse traditions to create something uniquely suited to modern needs. This exploration delves into how these modern rituals are constructed, their varied sources of inspiration, and their pivotal roles in their practitioners' spiritual lives.

The Genesis of Modern Rituals

Have you ever wondered where new spiritual rituals come from? In the tapestry of modern spirituality, new rituals often emerge from a melting pot of cultural and religious influences. For instance, New Age movements frequently incorporate elements from Eastern spiritualities, indigenous practices, and Western esoteric traditions to form ceremonies that address universal themes such as healing, renewal, and personal growth. These rituals are not just created; they are crafted, often with a conscious effort to be inclusive and resonate with a globally connected audience.

Crafting Inclusive Spaces

One of the defining characteristics of modern spiritual rituals is their emphasis on inclusivity. Interfaith ceremonies, for example, blend symbols, prayers, and practices from multiple religions to create a shared spiritual experience that honors the diversity of its participants. Such ceremonies might combine reading from the Bhagavad Gita with lighting candles for Sabbath, set to the sound of a Native American drum circle, creating a rich, multi-layered ritual that transcends individual religious boundaries.

Why does this matter? In today's world, where traditional religious affiliations are on the decline, especially among younger generations, these inclusive rituals offer a way to engage with spirituality that respects individual beliefs and backgrounds while fostering a sense of community and shared human values.

Personal Spiritual Expression

Modern rituals often prioritize personal expression and direct experience of the divine over rigid adherence to established doctrines. This shift reflects a broader cultural movement towards personal autonomy and self-definition. In New Age practices, for instance, participants might create their own rituals using personal significance elements, such as crystals, tarot cards, or even elements borrowed from pop culture. These personal rituals allow individuals to connect with the spiritual in ways that are meaningful and empowering to them personally.

How do these personalized practices impact spiritual communities? They can lead to a more dynamic and flexible community structure, where individual experiences and insights are valued as contributions to the collective understanding of the spiritual.

Contemporary Roles of Modern Rituals

The roles of modern rituals extend beyond personal and communal spirituality into broader societal contexts. Many of these practices are designed to address contemporary issues such as environmental awareness, social justice, and mental health. For example, rituals that focus on healing the Earth unite participants in environmental activism through a spiritual lens, while those centered on social justice can provide a powerful space for healing and solidarity among marginalized groups.

Moreover, in a world where mental health is increasingly a concern, rituals that promote mindfulness and emotional well-being are becoming more prevalent. These practices serve spiritual purposes and support psychological health, illustrating the adaptability of modern rituals to meet contemporary needs.

Part IV: Spiritual Paths to Personal Growth

Chapter 9: Overcoming Challenges Through Spirituality

Life is a journey often marked by trials and tribulations, and during these times, many find solace and strength in spirituality. This enduring aspect of human experience provides comfort and profound guidance as we navigate the complexities of life. This chapter delves into how various spiritual practices and beliefs can be instrumental in overcoming life's challenges, enhancing resilience, and fostering profound personal growth.

Whether grappling with mental health issues, coping with loss and grief, or seeking peace in chaotic times, spirituality offers a refuge and a framework for understanding and processing our experiences. The practices discussed in this chapter—from meditation and prayer to engaging with spiritual communities—are more than just rituals; they are pathways that lead to healing, understanding, and, sometimes, transformative growth.

This chapter explores the therapeutic aspects of spiritual practices. How can meditation, prayer, and community involvement alleviate symptoms of depression, anxiety, and stress? Here, we look at the evidence and hear stories highlighting spirituality's benefits in enhancing mental wellbeing.

Loss is a universal experience, and spiritual traditions provide unique comforts and perspectives in dealing with it. What roles do rituals and beliefs play in helping individuals process grief? We examine how these practices support the bereaved, fostering connections that transcend even death.

Often, our greatest challenges lead to the most significant spiritual and personal growth. How does adversity foster this development? This section will discuss the notion of post-traumatic growth from a spiritual viewpoint, showcasing how personal trials can deepen one's spiritual path and life purpose.

In an ever-turbulent world, finding inner stability is paramount. What spiritual techniques can help maintain peace of mind amid external upheaval? We explore practices like mindfulness and spiritual contemplation that help anchor the spirit during times of crisis.

Life's major transitions—be it a career change, relocation, or significant family milestones—often call for guidance. How can spiritual teachings and community support assist during these times? This discussion focuses on the role of spiritual advisors and sacred texts in providing direction and reassurance through life's significant changes.

In this chapter, we aim to illustrate the diversity of spiritual tools available to help us overcome life's obstacles and celebrate the profound capacity of spirituality to bring about healing and transformation. Through personal anecdotes, expert insights, and an exploration of various spiritual traditions, we uncover how spirituality enriches and empowers our lives, particularly in times of need.

The Transformative Power of Spirituality on Mental Health

Have you ever wondered how moments of quiet reflection or a heartfelt prayer can change the course of your day? Across the globe, countless individuals turn to spiritual practices as essential tools for managing their mental health. This exploration delves into the profound connection between spirituality and mental well-being, revealing how practices such as meditation, prayer, and active participation in spiritual communities can significantly alleviate psychological distress and enhance life's quality.

Modern research is increasingly acknowledging what many cultures have long appreciated: spirituality is a potent ally in the battle against mental illness. Numerous studies indicate that regular engagement in spiritual practices is correlated with better mental health outcomes, including lower levels of stress, anxiety, and depression. But what is it about these practices that offer such profound therapeutic benefits?

Meditation, often regarded as the cornerstone of spiritual practice, offers more than a momentary pause in our hectic lives. It trains the mind to achieve sustained focus, cultivates a heightened state of awareness, and promotes deep emotional peace. The process of mindfulness meditation, for example, encourages individuals to observe their thoughts and feelings without judgment, helping to break the cycle of chronic stress and anxiety. Clinical studies have shown that regular meditation can alter the brain's neural pathways, making you more resilient to stressors. Isn't it remarkable that we can rewire our brains and transform our mental health by simply sitting in silence?

Regardless of religious affiliation, prayer often acts as a profound source of comfort and strength. It allows individuals to express their fears, hopes, and gratitude, fostering a sense of security and stability. Prayer can lead to a powerful emotional release, offering a unique form of emotional cleansing that is difficult to find elsewhere. Have you ever felt a wave of relief wash over you after a heartfelt prayer? This emotional response is not just psychological; it's a profound interaction between our spiritual beliefs and our mental faculties, providing a buffer against the trials of life.

Spiritual communities offer unique social support, vital for maintaining mental health. These communities provide a sense of belonging, identity, and shared purpose. Whether it's attending a church service, participating in a meditation group, or engaging in a religious festival, being part of a spiritual community can reduce feelings of isolation and increase feelings of social connectedness and support. This communal aspect of spirituality can be especially beneficial for those suffering from loneliness, which is often a precursor to many psychological disorders.

Beyond the statistics and clinical studies, the anecdotes of individuals who have found solace and recovery through spirituality speak volumes. Consider the story of John, who after battling severe depression for years, found respite in Buddhist meditation practices. Or Mary, who overcame her anxiety through regular prayer and participation in her local church activities. These stories are not just testimonials; they are real-life examples of how spirituality can be a lifeline in the darkest of times.

Emotional resilience is perhaps one of the most significant benefits offered by spiritual practices. By fostering a deeper sense of meaning and connection, spirituality can help individuals navigate through life's ups and downs with grace and fortitude. It teaches acceptance, encourages forgiveness, and builds hope—all crucial elements for facing life's challenges with resilience rather than despair.

Incorporating spirituality into our lives can be a game-changer in our pursuit of mental wellness. Whether through meditation, prayer, or community involvement, the spiritual dimension offers ancient and profoundly effective tools. As we face various challenges in life, let us remember that spirituality is not just about seeking solace; it's about finding a deeper sense of peace, purpose, and connection. So why not explore these practices and see what changes you can bring into your own life?

As you reflect on this discussion, consider how you can integrate these spiritual practices into your daily routine. Could spirituality be the key that unlocks a more peaceful, resilient version of yourself?

Spiritual Practices in Grieving and Healing

Grief is a journey often walked in shadows, yet many find light and solace through the corridors of spirituality. How do various spiritual traditions guide us through the loss of a loved one? This exploration delves into the rituals, beliefs, and communal supports embedded in different faiths that provide comfort and help individuals find deeper meaning and continuity after a loss. In doing so, spirituality offers a bridge between the past and the potential for future healing.

The Role of Rituals in Mourning

Rituals serve as a powerful antidote to the chaos of grief. They offer structure during the disorienting days following a loss. For instance, in Christianity, the funeral service is a ritualized farewell, incorporating readings, hymns, and prayers that affirm the deceased's return to God, offering solace to those left behind. Have you ever felt a calming presence amidst the ritual of saying goodbye?

Similarly, in Islam, the Janazah prayer gathers the community to pray for the deceased, emphasizing life's transient nature and the eternal life to come. This communal prayer unites the mourners in their grief and reinforces the collective faith in divine wisdom.

Memorial Services Across Cultures

Across the globe, memorial services vary but share the common goal of honouring the deceased. In Hindu tradition, the Shraadh ceremony is performed annually as a tribute to the deceased's soul, believed to aid their journey in the afterlife and keep their memory alive in the family lineage. These rituals provide a set time and space to remember loved ones, which can be incredibly grounding for those who feel adrift in their sorrow.

Spiritual Counseling: Guiding the Bereaved

Spiritual leaders often play a crucial role in the healing process by providing counseling that reflects religious teachings on life, death, and the afterlife. This spiritual guidance can help individuals frame their loss within a broader existential perspective, fostering a sense of peace and acceptance. For example, Buddhist monks may offer teachings on impermanence and the nature of suffering, helping mourners understand and integrate the loss into their spiritual journey.

The support of a spiritual community can be particularly impactful during times of grief. These communities act as extended families, providing emotional support, practical help, and a sense of belonging. In Jewish traditions, the practice of sitting Shiva involves a week-long period of mourning where friends and family gather with the bereaved, sharing stories and prayers, thus enveloping the grieving individuals in a warm embrace of communal solidarity.

Finding Meaning After Loss

How do we continue bonds with those who have passed? Many spiritual practices endorse the ongoing relationship with the deceased through symbolic interactions. In Mexican culture, the Day of the Dead festivities see families decorate altars with the favourite foods and belongings of the deceased, a practice that joyously reaffirms the ongoing presence of lost loved ones in the lives of the living.

Interestingly, when navigated through spiritual lenses, grief can lead to significant personal growth and transformation. Engaging in spiritual practices such as meditation and prayer can foster an inner dialogue that might lead to new insights into the nature of life and personal strength. This transformation is often reflected in increased empathy towards others' suffering and a renewed commitment to living one's values.

Grief is an undeniable part of the human experience, but the potential for profound spiritual renewal and deeper connection lies within it. Through the structured compassion of rituals, the wisdom of spiritual counseling, and the supportive presence of community, individuals are guided gently through their darkest times. As we reflect on these spiritual pathways, we find solace and a beacon of hope that guides us towards healing and peace.

Spiritual Growth Through Adversity

Why do some spiritually profound insights come during the most challenging times? Adversity, often feared and avoided, holds a paradoxical power to deepen our spiritual lives and enhance our understanding of existence. This exploration delves into how confronting and overcoming difficulties can catalyze significant spiritual growth, often referred to as post-traumatic growth in psychological terms, but here considered from a spiritual perspective. Through personal anecdotes and teachings, we will uncover the transformative potential of faith and resilience in the face of life's trials.

The Phenomenon of Spiritual Growth Through Adversity

Post-traumatic growth refers to positive psychological change experienced as a result of adversity and other challenges, which is crucial for achieving a higher level of functioning. From a spiritual viewpoint, this concept transcends mere coping mechanisms, suggesting that individuals can experience profound spiritual awakenings through struggles. How do these awakenings occur, and what forms might they take? The answer lies in transforming the spiritual self as individuals seek meaning and reassurance in higher powers or deeper existential reflections.

Faith often becomes a refuge for those battered by life's storms. It provides comfort and a framework for giving adversity meaning and purpose. Consider the story of Malika, a cancer survivor whose ordeal brought her closer to her spiritual beliefs. She found in her faith solace and a renewed zest for life, claiming that her journey through illness taught her to appreciate every moment and see the divine in everyday existence. Isn't it remarkable how faith can transform the darkest episodes of our lives into chapters of insight and empowerment?

Stories of Resilience: Learning from Those Who Endured

Every culture and spiritual tradition has its tales of resilience—stories of individuals who faced overwhelming odds and emerged spiritually enriched. These narratives often serve as guideposts for others undergoing similar challenges. For instance, the Biblical story of Job, who endured tremendous suffering yet maintained his faith, inspires many to view their struggles through a spiritual lens, finding purpose and eventual redemption in their pain.

In more recent times, figures such as Nelson Mandela and Malala Yousafzai embody the principle of overcoming adversity through spiritual strength. Mandela's long imprisonment led him to a profound belief in forgiveness and reconciliation, principles that guided his later leadership and humanitarian efforts. Malala's bravery and recovery, underpinned by her deep spiritual and ethical convictions, have inspired a global movement for girls' education. What can we learn from such figures about the power of spiritual resilience?

Deepening Spiritual Awareness and Purpose

Adversity challenges our notions of purpose and success, often prompting a re-evaluation of what truly matters in life. This introspection can lead to a deeper spiritual awareness, where one's life purpose is viewed in terms of personal achievement and contributions to a greater good. How often do we consider our roles within the wider universe during times of peace, and how might our perspectives change when faced with trials?

Engaging in spiritual practices such as meditation, reflective prayer, or scriptural study can facilitate this transformation by fostering heightened awareness and connectedness to the divine. These practices help individuals cope with their circumstances and transcend them, cultivating a spiritual perspective that views adversities as opportunities for growth and learning.

As we navigate life's complexities, embracing adversity's spiritual dimensions can open doors to new understandings and profound growth. By acknowledging the transformative potential of our trials and turning to spiritual practices and communities for support, we can emerge from our challenges unbroken, enriched, and invigorated. In this light, adversity becomes not just an obstacle to be overcome but a vital part of our spiritual journey, refining us like gold through fire and leaving us with a clearer vision of who we are and what we are meant to do.

Embracing Spirituality Amidst Chaos

How often do we find ourselves overwhelmed by the tumultuous waves of life's chaos? Maintaining inner peace can sometimes feel daunting, whether it's a global pandemic, societal unrest, or personal crises. Yet, spirituality offers a beacon of hope, providing tools to weather these storms and emerge from them with more profound tranquility and understanding.

The Power of Mindfulness in Chaotic Times

In the eye of the storm, mindfulness teaches us to anchor ourselves in the present moment. But what does it mean to practice mindfulness when the world around us seems spinning out of control? Mindfulness involves observing our current experiences without judgment—acknowledging feelings, thoughts, and sensations as they are. This practice helps reduce anxiety and stress by preventing over-engagement with distressing thoughts or worries about the future.

Consider the example of Ella, a healthcare worker during the COVID-19 pandemic. Faced with daily challenges and high stress, Ella began practicing mindfulness to manage her anxiety. Through techniques learned in mindfulness meditation, she found herself better equipped to handle the emotional ups and downs of her demanding job, maintaining a calmness that also benefited her colleagues and patients.

Meditative Prayer: Solace in Sacred Words

Meditative prayer involves a deeper dialogue with the divine, where repetitive prayers or mantras focus and soothe the mind. This form of spiritual practice fosters a sense of peace and connects us with a higher power, offering comfort and guidance. How does the act of surrendering our fears to a greater force help stabilize our internal world?

Take the story of Michael, who turned to meditative prayer during a period of intense personal loss and uncertainty. Through his daily practice, he found the strength to accept his situation and experienced profound emotional healing, illustrating how spiritual engagement can transform despair into serenity and acceptance.

Spiritual Contemplation: Finding Depth in Silence

Spiritual contemplation involves deep, reflective thinking about one's life and beliefs, often in silence. This practice allows individuals to step back from the chaos and gain clarity about what truly matters. In times of global crisis, such as during social unrest or environmental threats, contemplation can help individuals align their actions with their values, leading to a more purposeful approach to life's challenges.

Sarah is an environmental activist who uses spiritual contemplation to maintain her equilibrium amidst the often overwhelming fight against climate change. Through her contemplative practices, she finds the resilience to continue her work, driven by a clear understanding of her role in the larger context of life.

As we navigate through the storms of life, the spiritual tools of mindfulness, meditative prayer, and contemplation offer more than just a refuge—they provide a framework for growth and resilience. These practices empower us to maintain our balance amidst chaos, ensuring that we endure and thrive. They remind us that within each of us lies an unshakeable centre, a place of peace that can weather any storm. In embracing these spiritual practices, we find solace and a profound connection to the enduring human spirit that unites us all in the face of adversity.

As you reflect on these insights, consider how you might incorporate these spiritual practices into your life. What storms might you calm with the gentle power of spirituality?

Navigating Life's Transitions with Spiritual Insight

Change, while a constant in life, often brings a mix of excitement and anxiety. Whether it's starting a new job, moving to a different city, getting married, or welcoming a child, these major life transitions can unsettle even the sturdiest of souls. How can spiritual teachings and community support guide and reassure during these pivotal moments? This exploration delves into the ways spiritual advisors, community networks, and sacred texts can serve as compasses during life's significant transitions, helping individuals navigate change with grace and confidence.

Spiritual advisors, be they priests, rabbis, imams, gurus, or monks, often bring deep religious knowledge and years of experience in counseling their followers through life's ups and downs. How do these figures use their wisdom to guide others? Consider the story of Father Michael, a parish priest who has been instrumental in guiding his congregants through marriage preparations, offering practical advice and spiritual wisdom on the sacrament of matrimony.

Individual counseling sessions with spiritual leaders can provide tailored guidance that resonates deeply with personal circumstances. These sessions often help individuals reflect on their life choices in alignment with their spiritual values, offering a clearer vision of the path ahead. Anecdotes of people who have found profound insights during such sessions highlight how personalized spiritual guidance can transform anxiety into action.

Spiritual communities often act as extended families that provide emotional support and practical help during major transitions. How does this communal support manifest? For example, when someone moves to a new city, local community members might help them settle in, providing both friendship and necessary local knowledge, thereby easing the stress of relocation.

Communal rituals and celebrations, such as wedding ceremonies, baby christenings, or farewell gatherings, mark life's milestones and reinforce communal bonds. These events are steeped in spiritual significance and are supported by collective joy and blessing, reinforcing the individual's sense of belonging and acceptance during times of change.

Sacred texts like the Bible, Quran, Bhagavad Gita, and others are replete with stories, parables, and teachings that address the very essence of human experience—including change and transition. How do these texts guide individuals in modern times? Extracts from these scriptures can offer comfort and direction, providing timeless wisdom on how to handle new challenges and opportunities.

The stories of biblical figures like Moses, who led the Israelites out of Egypt, or of Arjuna in the Bhagavad Gita, facing his inner doubts on the battlefield, are powerful examples of navigating challenging transitions with faith and courage. These stories not only provide a scriptural basis for enduring change but also offer inspirational models that resonate with individuals facing similar uncertainties.

As we navigate different phases of life, the interplay of spiritual mentorship, community support, and the profound wisdom of sacred texts can provide a formidable support system. By engaging with these spiritual resources, individuals are better equipped to face the uncertainties of life transitions, not merely surviving them but growing through them. In the embrace of spirituality, we find not just guidance but also the reassurance that we are not alone in our journeys. As you face your next life transition, consider how you might connect more deeply with your spiritual side to guide and enrich your path forward.

In navigating life's inevitable changes, may we all find solace in spirituality, drawing from its deep wells of wisdom to face the future with hope and heart.

Chapter 10: Ethics and Morality in Spiritual Life

In the journey of human existence, ethics and morality stand out as the threads that hold together the fabric of societies and cultures. These principles guide individual actions and shape communal life, setting standards for what is deemed right and wrong. But where do these standards come from? For countless individuals worldwide, the answers lie within the spiritual and religious traditions they follow.

This chapter digs into the profound connection between spirituality and moral conduct, exploring how various religious beliefs and spiritual practices inform, influence, and inspire the ethical landscapes of their adherents. From the ancient scriptures of world religions to the lived experiences of their followers, we will explore how spiritual teachings help carve paths of righteousness and morality, guiding individuals in their daily lives and interactions.

As we navigate this exploration, we will examine the ethical teachings at the heart of major world religions such as Christianity, Islam, Buddhism, Hinduism, and Judaism. We will uncover how commandments, precepts, and moral codes such as the Christian Ten Commandments, the Islamic Sharia, the Buddhist Five Precepts, the Hindu concept of Dharma, and the Jewish laws of the Torah not only prescribe specific actions but also cultivate virtues that lay the foundation for a moral life.

Moreover, we will examine how these spiritual guidelines adapt to contemporary issues, influencing modern ethical debates and helping adherents navigate complex moral landscapes in an ever-evolving world. Through this examination, we aim to understand the role of spirituality in fostering ethical awareness and moral responsibility, highlighting how deeply intertwined our spiritual beliefs are with our moral actions.

Ethical Teachings Across World Religions

How do we discern right from wrong in a world of diverse beliefs and cultures? The answer often lies in the rich tapestry of religious teachings that have guided humanity for millennia. These religions—Christianity, Islam, Buddhism, Hinduism, and Judaism—not only foster spiritual growth but also mold ethical landscapes, influencing the moral decisions of their followers. How do these faiths articulate their core ethical principles, and what can we learn from their moral codes?

Christianity: The Ten Commandments

At the core of Christian ethics are the Ten Commandments, foundational moral directives received by Moses at Mount Sinai. These commandments encompass obligations to God—like keeping the Sabbath holy—and duties to other people, such as honouring one's parents and refraining from theft and falsehood. Have you ever considered how these ancient dictates influence modern legal and ethical norms worldwide?

Beyond the commandments, the teachings of Jesus, particularly in the Sermon on the Mount, provide profound insights into Christian morality, emphasizing values like mercy, purity, and peace. These teachings challenge believers to reach beyond simple legalism into the depths of ethical altruism. How might these principles translate into everyday actions in today's world?

Islam: The Sharia Law

In Islam, Sharia, derived from the Quran and the Hadiths, offers a detailed framework for living a moral life that covers every aspect of daily existence—from family life and business dealings to spiritual practices and social responsibilities. Sharia promotes welfare and prevents harm, ensuring justice, fairness, and human dignity. How does this holistic approach impact the followers' actions and societal structures?

Integral to Islamic ethics are the Five Pillars, which encapsulate core practices and principles guiding moral and spiritual discipline. These include not only acts of worship but also Zakat (charity), which underscores the moral obligation to help others, reinforcing the community's bond through compassion and care.

Buddhism: The Five Precepts

Buddhism offers the Five Precepts as basic ethical guidelines that lay the groundwork for a life free from harm and suffering. These precepts prohibit killing, stealing, sexual misconduct, lying, and intoxication. Each precept nurtures the development of a compassionate, truthful, and mindful mind. How do these principles support the Buddhist goal of overcoming suffering?

Hinduism: The Concept of Dharma

In Hinduism, Dharma encompasses duty, righteousness, and moral law—guiding individual actions and the entire cosmic order. It is both universal and personal, dictating that one's duty varies according to their age, occupation, and station in life. How does this flexible yet rigorous concept help individuals navigate the complexities of life while maintaining moral integrity?

Judaism: The Torah's Laws

Judaism grounds its ethical teachings in the Torah, which includes detailed laws covering all aspects of life. These laws are religious directives and a comprehensive legal system that includes charity, justice, honesty, and social responsibility. How do these laws foster a sense of community and social justice among Jewish people?

While the ethical teachings of these religions are rooted in diverse theological frameworks, they all aim to guide adherents towards a life of morality and integrity. These religions offer a set of rules and a way to make sense of the world, improve human interactions, and achieve personal peace. By exploring these foundational ethical principles, we gain a deeper understanding of each faith and a greater appreciation for the universal quest for morality and justice that binds humanity. In embracing these principles, one finds guidance for personal conduct and inspiration for building a more ethical and compassionate world.

The Spiritual Response to Ethical Dilemmas

How do age-old spiritual teachings apply to the breakneck pace of modern technological and environmental challenges? From the genetic modification of organisms to the integration of artificial intelligence in daily life, and the pressing urgency of environmental conservation, today's ethical dilemmas are complex and multifaceted. This exploration delves into how different spiritual traditions bring their ancient wisdom to bear on these contemporary issues, offering insights that aim to guide adherents through the moral maze of the modern world.

Genetic Engineering: Modifying Life's Blueprint

The prospect of genetically modified organisms (GMOs) raises significant ethical questions about the sanctity and integrity of natural life. How do different spiritual perspectives view the manipulation of life's genetic structure? Christianity often considers these advancements with cautious scrutiny, emphasizing the sanctity of creation, whereas Hinduism might frame such interventions within the laws of Karma, pondering the consequences of such actions on the soul's journey.

Consider the response to genetically modified crops designed to withstand drought in regions plagued by famine. While the technological solution addresses immediate needs, spiritual perspectives might raise questions about long-term impacts and the ethical considerations of 'playing God'. How do we balance these needs and beliefs? The answers vary significantly across different faiths, providing a rich tapestry of moral reasoning.

Artificial Intelligence: The Soul of the Machine

As artificial intelligence becomes increasingly sophisticated, questions arise about consciousness, sentience, and the responsibilities of creators towards their creations. Jewish ethical teachings, deeply analytical, often approach AI with questions about the imitation of life and the boundaries of human dominion as prescribed in the Torah. Meanwhile, Buddhist philosophy might explore the implications of non-sentient beings performing roles that require compassion and wisdom, traditionally human attributes.

Anecdotes from tech developers integrating AI in healthcare— where decisions about life and death can potentially be delegated to algorithms—highlight the need for an ethical framework informed by compassion and respect for life, principles deeply rooted in many spiritual traditions.

Environmental Stewardship: Caring for Creation

Environmental issues offer perhaps the most direct call to action for contemporary spiritual communities. Many religions see the Earth as a sacred trust granted to humanity. For example, Pope Francis's encyclical, Laudato Si', is a powerful call within Catholicism to protect our "common home." In Islam, the concept of "Khalifa," or stewardship, implores Muslims to protect and preserve nature as caretakers of God's creation.

Engaging stories from faith-based initiatives, such as the interfaith solar power projects that unite communities around sustainable energy, demonstrate how spiritual teachings inspire concrete actions that address modern ecological crises. These initiatives not only solve physical problems but also foster a sense of spiritual fulfillment and communal unity.

In confronting the ethical challenges posed by modernity, the ancient wisdom of spiritual traditions provides a moral compass and a source of comfort and inspiration. These teachings encourage reflection, provoke dialogue, and inspire action, ensuring that as humanity progresses, it does so with consideration and compassion. By integrating spiritual perspectives into discussions on genetic engineering, artificial intelligence, and environmental care, we enrich the discourse and potentially find more holistic and harmonious solutions to these pressing dilemmas.

As we continue to navigate these complex issues, let us consider the vast reservoir of spiritual wisdom that has guided humanity for centuries. Could these age-old teachings hold the keys to unlocking ethical solutions for the future? Let us draw on this wisdom to question and act with moral clarity and spiritual insight.

Interfaith Dialogues on Universal Moral Values

What binds us together in our human experience? Across diverse landscapes and through myriad cultural lenses, the quest for understanding and implementing truth, justice, equality, and peace forms the cornerstone of our moral compass. How do different faiths approach these universal moral issues, and what can we learn from their perspectives to foster a more harmonious world? This exploration delves into the interfaith perspectives, illuminating commonalities and celebrating the differences in our collective ethical inquiries.

Truthfulness is revered across all major religions as a fundamental virtue. Christianity upholds truth through Jesus' teachings, proclaiming "the truth will set you free" (John 8:32), a call echoed in the Islamic tradition which considers honesty not just a virtue but a direct reflection of one's faithfulness. How do such teachings influence their followers' everyday decisions and life views?

Engaging anecdotes from interfaith dialogues, such as a conference where a Buddhist monk and a Jewish rabbi discussed the role of truth in fostering inner peace and societal harmony, highlight how mutual understanding can lead to enriched perspectives on maintaining integrity in a complex world.

Justice, a concept as old as civilization itself, takes on varied dimensions in different religious contexts. The Hindu concept of 'Karma' underpins a cosmic sense of justice, where one's actions determine their future fate. In contrast, the Islamic Sharia emphasizes justice as a communal duty, vital for societal wellness. How do these views influence the actions and policies supported by these communities?

Case studies from initiatives like interfaith charity organizations and justice reform programs led by religious coalitions provide practical examples of how spiritual doctrines guide actions that aim for fair treatment and equitable opportunities for all.

Equality, especially regarding human rights and gender equality, is addressed distinctly within various faiths. While some critics point to religious doctrines as perpetuating inequality, many religious groups have pioneered for equal rights, using their scriptures for support. For example, many Christian denominations advocate for gender equality based on Galatians 3:28, "There is neither Jew nor Greek, slave nor free, male nor female, for you are all one in Christ Jesus."

Illustrations from interfaith panels that discuss women's roles in religion and society can demonstrate how religious communities can evolve and respond to contemporary calls for equality, often leading to breakthroughs in traditional roles within religious leadership and community structures.

Peace is perhaps the most universally aspired-to ideal within spiritual doctrines. Buddhism's ahimsa (non-harm) principle aligns closely with Christianity's beatitude, "Blessed are the peacemakers." These teachings foster a culture of peace that transcends individual faiths, leading to collaborative peace-building efforts in conflict zones worldwide.

Stories from peace missions involving multiple faiths, such as joint humanitarian efforts in war-torn areas, not only put these principles into action but also show the power of united spiritual convictions in making tangible changes towards global peace.

In our exploration of interfaith perspectives on universal moral issues, we uncover more than just philosophical ideals; we discover the practical power of these principles in shaping a just, equal, and peaceful world. By engaging in these dialogues, we enrich our spiritual understanding and contribute to a collective moral framework that respects diversity while striving for unity. As we continue these conversations, let us remember that each faith, with its unique approach to ethics and morality, contributes valuable insights to our shared human experience, building bridges that connect us across all divides.

Infusing Spirituality into Business Ethics

What happens when business meets spirituality? In today's highly competitive and often cutthroat market, integrating spiritual and moral principles into business practices is refreshing and revolutionary. This article explores how ethical leadership, informed by deep spiritual values, can transform corporate cultures, enhance stakeholder relations, and redefine corporate social responsibility. How do leaders weave their spiritual beliefs into the fabric of their business decisions, and what impact does this have on their companies and society at large?

Spiritual ethics in business transcends traditional profit-driven strategies, introducing a holistic approach that considers well-being, integrity, and purpose as pivotal as financial success. But what does spiritual ethics look like in practice? It involves principles such as honesty, compassion, fairness, and responsibility being embedded into every business decision, from client interactions to partnership agreements.

Consider the CEO who meditates daily and uses this practice to foster a calm, clear mindset when making strategic decisions. This leader's commitment to mindfulness benefits personal well-being and enhances the ethical quality of their leadership, promoting a more thoughtful and inclusive approach to business management.

One notable example is a tech startup in Silicon Valley led by a CEO deeply influenced by Buddhist teachings on compassion and non-harm. This leader has implemented policies that prioritize employee wellness and environmental responsibility, significantly reducing the company's carbon footprint and increasing employee satisfaction and retention rates. How does this reflect on the company's performance and public perception?

Another case is that of a family-owned enterprise in the UK, where the management practices Quaker principles, emphasizing honesty, transparency, and community service. These principles have shaped the company's interactions with suppliers, customers, and employees, fostering long-term relationships built on trust and mutual respect. This approach has enhanced their reputation and resulted in consistent growth despite economic downturns.

Spiritual ethics often drive businesses to go beyond conventional philanthropy, leading to initiatives that sustainably impact communities. For instance, a manufacturing company might use a portion of its profits to fund renewable energy projects in underserved regions, not just as charity but as part of a spiritual commitment to stewardship of the earth.

Highlighting leaders who embody spiritual principles in their professional roles is a powerful model for upcoming entrepreneurs and established businesspersons. These leaders demonstrate that achieving success without compromising ethical values is possible, encouraging a new generation to consider how their work can contribute positively to the world.

Incorporating spirituality into business ethics offers a profound way to rethink the role of commerce in society. It challenges the stereotype of business as solely profit-driven and presents an alternative where companies operate as communities of purpose. By aligning business practices with spiritual and moral principles, leaders can create enterprises that prosper and contribute to the welfare of all stakeholders—employees, communities, and the environment.

As we reflect on these insights, consider how integrating spiritual values into your professional life could reshape your business approach and your impact on the world. Could the future of business lie in a greater convergence of spirituality and corporate practice? With ethical leadership at the helm, the potential for positive change is limitless.

How Personal Morality Shapes Community Wellbeing

What happens when the private virtues of individuals spill over into the public sphere? In a world where headlines often highlight division and despair, the impact of personal morality on community wellbeing provides a refreshing counter-narrative. This exploration delves into how the moral and ethical practices advocated by various spiritual traditions sculpt individuals' character and enhance the health and cohesion of entire communities. How significant is the role of individual virtue in fostering a thriving society?

Across religions and spiritual paths, teachings on charity, altruism, and community service are prominent. These principles are lofty ideals and practical guidelines that affect everyday interactions and decisions. For instance, the concept of 'Zakat' in Islam isn't merely a charitable donation; it's a duty to support the community's welfare. Similarly, the Buddhist practice of 'Metta' (loving-kindness) extends beyond personal meditation to actual interactions within the community. How do these practices manifest in the lives of the faithful?

Consider the story of Maria, a devout Christian in the Philippines, whose weekly routine includes organizing food drives for less fortunate members of her neighborhood. Inspired by the Biblical injunction to "love thy neighbor," her actions ripple through her community, fostering a spirit of generosity and mutual support. What does this tell us about the power of individual actions rooted in spiritual values?

Charitable acts and community service are common threads in the fabric of religious teachings, but their impact extends beyond immediate relief. When individuals engage in these practices, they often set in motion a virtuous cycle that strengthens the bonds of the community. This section explores various case studies where communities transformed economically, socially, and spiritually through organized acts of charity and service.

Spiritual organizations often act as catalysts for community development by channeling individual virtues into collective action. Examples include faith-based initiatives that have built schools, hospitals, and housing in underserved areas. These projects provide essential services and create a sense of shared purpose and community solidarity.

Research shows that communities with high levels of civic engagement and interpersonal trust tend to have better health outcomes, lower crime rates, and higher educational achievements. This section would delve into studies linking these outcomes with the prevalence of moral and ethical practices derived from spiritual teachings.

From a small town in Sweden where church groups play an integral role in integrating refugees into community life, to a village in India where Hindu teachings on 'Seva' (selfless service) have led to successful environmental conservation projects, these stories highlight how spirituality-inspired morality can lead to substantial community benefits.

In examining the profound connection between personal morality and community wellbeing, it becomes clear that each individual's ethical choices can contribute significantly to societal health. The teachings of various spiritual traditions guide individual behaviour and inspire a culture of compassion and cooperation that underpins a healthy society. As we reflect on these insights, we are reminded of the potential within each person not just to live a morally upright life but to elevate the entire community. As these virtues ripple outward, they reinforce the foundation of a society that is not only functioning but flourishing.

In embracing these principles, may we all aspire to be catalysts for positive change, proving that virtue is not just a personal good, but a communal treasure. What role will you play in weaving the moral fabric of your community?

Elena Ray

The Power of Forgiveness and Reconciliation

What makes forgiveness one of the most powerful acts a human can perform? Across cultures and religions, forgiveness is seen as a moral duty and a profound catalyst for personal healing and community harmony. This exploration delinks into the spiritual teachings on forgiveness and reconciliation, examining how these principles facilitate profound transformations and mend the fabric of relationships torn by conflict and misunderstanding.

Virtually every major religion holds forgiveness as a core value. Christianity preaches "forgive seventy-seven times" (Matthew 18:22), emphasizing limitless forgiveness. In Islam, the Quran extols the virtues of forgiveness, urging believers to pardon others to receive God's mercy. Buddhism sees forgiveness as essential to spiritual liberation, a release from anger and resentment.

Anecdotes from sacred texts and teachings illustrate forgiveness in action. The story of Joseph in the Hebrew Bible, who forgave his brothers for selling him into slavery, offers a powerful example of forgiveness and redemption, showing that healing is possible even when trust is deeply betrayed.

Personal stories of forgiveness often highlight its transformative power on the individual level. Consider the tale of a woman who forgave the drunk driver who injured her severely; her forgiveness liberated her from a prison of bitterness and allowed her to lead a full, compassionate life. How does releasing resentment change our inner world and our external interactions?

On a broader scale, forgiveness can be pivotal in community reconciliation. In post-apartheid South Africa, the Truth and Reconciliation Commission provided a platform for both victims and perpetrators of apartheid-era violence to express their experiences and seek forgiveness, facilitating national healing and peacebuilding. What can we learn from such large-scale forgiveness and reconciliation processes?

Forgiveness is rarely instantaneous; it is a process that often involves several stages, from acknowledging hurt and anger to understanding the offender's perspective and finally letting go of grievances. Spiritual traditions offer various practices to aid this process, including prayer, meditation, and rituals of atonement and healing.

How do communities foster an environment where forgiveness can flourish? Initiatives like community dialogues and peace circles can help individuals and groups navigate the challenges of forgiveness. These forums allow for open communication, mutual understanding, and the rebuilding of trust.

Forgiveness is not just an act but a way of living that continuously challenges and enriches those who practice it. By embracing forgiveness, individuals and communities release themselves from the chains of past grievances and open doors to new possibilities of understanding and cooperation. As we reflect on the teachings and stories of forgiveness, we are invited to consider its role in our lives. How might embracing forgiveness more fully enhance your personal peace and contribute to the well-being of your community?

In cultivating a spirit of forgiveness, we nurture a more compassionate and connected world, proving that even the deepest wounds can heal through the grace of understanding and the power of forgiveness.

The Liberating Power of Non-Attachment and Simplicity

In an era defined by consumerism and material excess, the spiritual teachings of non-attachment and simplicity offer a refreshing pathway to deeper contentment and ethical living. But what does it truly mean to live a life of simplicity and non-attachment? Across Buddhism, Christianity, and Hinduism, these principles are not about deprivation but discovering abundance in what truly matters. How do these ancient doctrines remain relevant in our modern lives, and what can they teach us about finding peace and purpose?

Buddhism teaches that attachment to material things and ephemeral desires leads to suffering. By practicing detachment, individuals can overcome the illusions that bind them to cycles of desire and disappointment. But isn't detachment often misunderstood as disengagement from the world?

Through the lens of Buddhist teachings, detachment is an active engagement in the world with a mindful simplicity that prioritizes inner peace over external accumulation. Examples abound of Buddhist practitioners and monks who embody this philosophy, showing that joy comes from appreciation and awareness, not accumulation.

The Christian tradition emphasizes simplicity as a form of devotion, citing Jesus' lifestyle and teachings that caution against the accumulation of wealth. The biblical exhortation that "it is easier for a camel to go through the eye of a needle than for someone who is rich to enter the kingdom of God" (Matthew 19:24) challenges followers to reconsider their priorities. How does this perspective encourage followers to live differently?

Stories from the Christian community, like those of modern minimalist movements inspired by faith, illustrate the pursuit of a life focused on spiritual richness rather than material wealth. These narratives often reveal a profound sense of freedom and clarity gained from this lifestyle choice.

In Hinduism, asceticism is not merely about renouncing worldly possessions but about achieving Moksha—liberation from the cycle of rebirth. This quest involves practices that might seem extreme but aim to deepen spiritual insight and detachment from physical and emotional attachments.

Hindu ascetics, or Sadhus, are often revered figures who remind society of the spiritual dimensions of existence. Their lives pose a rhetorical question to all: What truly binds you in life? Their presence acts as a living testament to the values of non-attachment and simplicity.

The teachings of non-attachment and simplicity from these diverse traditions offer profound insights into leading a fulfilled life. They remind us that in simplicity, we find the space to grow spiritually; in non-attachment, we find the freedom to experience life as it is.

As we navigate the complexities of modern living, adopting these principles can help us foster a sense of peace and ethical clarity. Whether through mindfulness practices inspired by Buddhism, the Christian focus on spiritual richness, or the Hindu pursuit of liberation, embracing these teachings can transform personal lives and community wellbeing. How might your life change if you chose to live more simply and detach from unnecessary excess?

By exploring and integrating these spiritual lessons, we enrich our lives and contribute to creating a more mindful and compassionate world. So, as you reflect on your own journey, consider what attachments might be holding you back from experiencing true freedom and peace.

Chapter 11: Exploring Your Spiritual Identity

In life's journey, few quests are as profound and enriching as exploring one's spiritual identity. This journey into the depths of what we believe, why we believe it, and how it shapes our lives is not just about uncovering a set of spiritual labels or practices—it's about connecting with the essence of our being." This chapter invites you on a reflective expedition to discover and articulate your unique spiritual path.

Why does spiritual identity matter? For many, it serves as the foundation of meaning in life, influencing decisions, shaping morals, and guiding interactions with others and the world. Understanding your spiritual identity can clarify your purpose, intensify your convictions, and enhance your peace of mind. It can transform how you perceive challenges, celebrate joys, and engage with the mysteries of existence.

However, exploring spiritual identity is no small task. It involves delving into personal beliefs, examining the influence of cultural and religious backgrounds, and being open to the evolution of your spiritual understanding. This chapter is designed to guide you through this introspective process, offering tools and reflections to help you map out your spiritual landscape. You will be encouraged to consider a spectrum of beliefs, identify practices that resonate deeply with you, and understand how your spirituality interacts with your communal and personal life.

From mapping the contours of your beliefs against the backdrop of world religions to integrating personalized spiritual practices into your daily routine, this chapter aims to equip you with the knowledge and insight to navigate your spiritual journey. Whether you are firmly rooted in a particular tradition or still searching for a spiritual home, this exploration is about honoring your unique path—understanding how it reflects your deepest values and can guide you towards greater fulfillment and peace.

Let us embark on this journey of discovery together, with open hearts and minds, ready to uncover the rich tapestry of beliefs and experiences that define our spiritual identities.

Unraveling Your Spiritual Identity

What shapes your sense of right and wrong? What beliefs anchor you in times of turmoil and guide your everyday decisions? These questions touch on something deep and defining: your spiritual identity. Unlike your social or professional identity, your spiritual identity taps into the fundamental beliefs and values that frame your understanding of the universe and your place within it. This exploration is not just about identifying with a religion or philosophy; it's about connecting with the core of your being and understanding how this influences every aspect of your life.

Spiritual identity embodies your deepest beliefs about existence, morality, and purpose. It encompasses the values and practices that arise from these beliefs and how they manifest in your daily life. But why is understanding your spiritual identity important? Because it informs your actions, molds your responses to life's challenges, and shapes your goals and aspirations. It's the bedrock upon which your life choices are made and is often the source of meaning and satisfaction in life.

How does one begin to explore such an intimate and complex aspect of themselves? The journey starts with reflection—examining the beliefs you hold, questioning their origins, and understanding how they align with your life's actions and choices. What do you find sacred, and why? How do these elements influence your view of the world?

For many, the journey into spiritual identity begins in childhood, deeply influenced by family beliefs and cultural traditions. From the bedtime stories told by your grandparents to the religious rituals observed in family gatherings, these experiences sow the seeds of spiritual identity. But as we grow older, we often reassess these inherited beliefs. Have you ever wondered whether your childhood beliefs still hold true for you?

The cultural environment also plays a significant role in shaping one's spiritual outlook. The societal norms, the prevailing philosophies, and even the national crises of one's homeland can profoundly influence one's spiritual beliefs and practices. Reflecting on how your culture has shaped your spiritual views can provide insights into the elements of your belief system that are uniquely yours versus those adopted from your surroundings.

Personal experiences, which test your limits or shake your foundations, can dramatically reshape your spiritual identity. Whether it's a near-death experience, the loss of a loved one, or a moment of unexpected revelation, such experiences can prompt profound questioning and growth in your spiritual life. How have your pivotal life events influenced your spiritual beliefs?

Our spiritual beliefs can evolve as we encounter new experiences and expand our horizons. This section would explore how to navigate the changes in your spiritual identity. Embracing flexibility in your spiritual journey allows for a more authentic expression of who you are in life's ever-changing landscape.

Understanding and embracing your spiritual identity is not a destination but a journey of continuous exploration and reflection. It's about building a narrative that resonates with who you are at your core and allows you to move through the world with a sense of purpose and peace. As you delve deeper into understanding your spiritual identity, consider how this exploration can enrich your life and relationships. What new paths might open up when you fully embrace your spiritual essence?

In this journey of self-discovery, every reflection, question, and insight adds to the mosaic of your spiritual identity, enhancing your own life and enriching the lives of those around you through deeper understanding and empathy.

A Journey Through Diverse Beliefs

In a world as diverse as ours, the variety of spiritual beliefs and practices is as vast as the ocean. Have you ever considered where your spiritual beliefs fit within this expansive panorama? Exploring the broad spectrum of spiritual beliefs enriches our understanding of the world and deepens our insight into our own spiritual identities. This journey through various faiths and philosophical systems introduces the concept of spiritual pluralism and offers a framework for mapping your personal spiritual landscape.

Spiritual pluralism is the recognition and acceptance that multiple paths can lead to spiritual truth. It acknowledges that no single religious or spiritual tradition holds a monopoly on truth. But what does this mean for individuals exploring their own beliefs? It suggests an openness to learning from various traditions, which can enrich one's spiritual journey.

Incorporating pluralism into your spiritual exploration encourages a broader understanding and respect for others' paths. This approach fosters tolerance and promotes a deeper self-reflection about why we choose certain beliefs over others. How might understanding others' beliefs challenge and refine your own?

This section offers an overview of major world religions—Christianity, Islam, Hinduism, Buddhism, Judaism—and newer spiritual movements like Baha'i, Scientology, and modern pagan practices. Each faith or belief system is presented with its core doctrines, rituals, and ethical teachings. What can the ancient wisdom of Buddhism teach us about mindfulness and suffering? How do Christian teachings on love and forgiveness challenge us to act in our daily lives?

Often overlooked, indigenous and folk religions offer profound insights into the spiritual connection with nature and community. Exploring these can reveal how deeply spirituality is woven into the fabric of daily life and survival, providing a contrast to more institutionalized religions.

How do you determine where your beliefs align within this spectrum? Simple exercises can help you identify your core beliefs and values. For instance, creating a belief map where you list down beliefs on various aspects like afterlife, the nature of divinity, the purpose of life, and ethical living can help you visually place where your convictions align with established religious doctrines.

Another useful exercise is the comparative reflection where you explore different beliefs and practices and note your reactions to them. Which beliefs resonate with you, and which challenge your existing views? This can be a revealing process that pushes you to think deeply about the origins and flexibility of your beliefs.

As you chart your way through the diverse landscapes of global spirituality, remember that the goal isn't just to categorize yourself within a spectrum but to understand more deeply why certain beliefs resonate with you. This exploration is less about finding definitive answers and more about continuing to ask the right questions.

How does your spiritual journey evolve as you learn more about others' beliefs? Does this exploration bring clarity or more questions? Either outcome is a step forward in your spiritual growth. Embrace the journey with openness, and let your discoveries enrich your spiritual outlook and your engagement with the world around you.

Balancing Personal Spirituality with Organized Religion

In the mosaic of modern spirituality, where does one find the balance between personal beliefs and the structured doctrines of organized religions? This is not merely a question of preference but a profound exploration of identity and belonging. As individuals navigate their spiritual journeys, they often encounter the challenge of aligning deeply personal spiritual insights with formal religions' broader, sometimes rigid frameworks. This article delves into the nuanced relationship between these two realms, exploring how to blend personal convictions with communal faith practices and the implications of choosing an independent spiritual path.

Personal spirituality is often described as an individual's unique, deeply personal relationship with the divine or the universe, shaped by personal experiences, reflections, and revelations. It is fluid, evolving, and intimately personal. In contrast, organized religions offer a communal belief system structured around shared doctrines, rituals, and moral codes, providing a collective identity and a sense of belonging to its adherents. How do these two dimensions interact, and can they coexist harmoniously within an individual?

For many, personal spirituality provides a freedom to explore and express their faith in ways that feel most authentic to their experiences and understandings. However, organized religions deliver a sense of community and shared history that can enrich an individual's spiritual life. Can one maintain personal beliefs while participating in broader religious practices without feeling conflicted?

Navigating the balance between personal spirituality and the teachings of a formal religion can be likened to walking a tightrope. Each step must be measured and deliberate, considering both the individual's inner convictions and the external expectations of the religious community. For instance, a Christian might find deep personal meaning in meditative practices more traditionally associated with Eastern religions, incorporating these into their prayer life without detracting from their Christian faith.

The challenges of this balance are not trivial. Individuals may face criticism or feel alienated from their religious communities for holding unconventional beliefs or practices. Conversely, the benefits of successfully integrating personal spirituality with organized religion can lead to a richer, more fulfilling spiritual experience. Examples of individuals who have navigated this path successfully can serve as both inspiration and guidance for others.

For some, the differences between personal spirituality and their religion's doctrines may be too great to reconcile. Individuals might choose a path entirely independent of any formal religious framework in these cases. What does this journey look like, and what are its inherent challenges and rewards?

Even outside the bounds of organized religion, community remains important. Many find new kinds of spiritual communities with others who share similar eclectic or individualized beliefs. Often informal and flexible, these communities can provide support and a sense of belonging without the constraints of traditional religious structures.

The journey between personal spirituality and organized religion is deeply personal and uniquely challenging. It requires courage to stay true to one's convictions while respectfully navigating the communal aspects of formal religious practices. Whether you find harmony within the structure of a religion or carve a solitary path, the key is to pursue an authentic and fulfilling spiritual life.

As you reflect on your spiritual identity, consider the values that resonate most deeply with you and the kind of spiritual community that will support your growth. Remember, the goal is not to fit a mold, but to forge a spiritual path that brings true peace and purpose to your life.

Choosing Practices That Speak to Your Soul

In the diverse landscape of spiritual traditions, we seek practices that resonate deeply with our inner selves. But how do you determine which spiritual practices align with your personal beliefs? And once identified, how can you incorporate these into your daily life to enhance your spiritual growth and wellbeing? This exploration is not just about adopting rituals; it's about enriching your spiritual journey with practices that truly reflect and nurture your soul.

Resonance in the context of spirituality refers to how well a practice aligns with your inner beliefs and feelings. It's that profound sense of connection and rightness you feel when a certain ritual or practice deeply aligns with your personal ethos. But why is resonance important? Because spiritual practices are meant to feed your soul, offering peace, grounding, and a deeper connection to the universe.

Begin with an open mind. Explore meditation from Buddhist traditions, prayer practices from Christian, Islamic, and Jewish teachings, physical yogic practices from Hinduism, and nature-centric rituals from indigenous and pagan traditions. What feelings do these evoke in you? Are you seeking tranquility, divine connection, physical alignment, or a deeper understanding of nature?

Meditation and mindfulness are among the most universally adaptable practices across spiritual traditions. Whether it's the mindfulness of Zen Buddhism, the prayerful meditation of the Rosary in Catholicism, or Sufi practices of heart-centered meditation, these practices help cultivate a state of awareness and peace. How can you adapt these practices to fit into your morning or evening routine?

Consider starting with five minutes of meditation each day, gradually increasing as you become more comfortable. Find a specific place in your home that helps you transition into a peaceful state more easily. This could be a small corner with a cushion, a candle, or even a view of a garden or the sky.

Many spiritual traditions emphasize the importance of connecting with the natural world. This could involve celebrating phases of the moon, solstices, and equinoxes. How can these celebrations enhance your connection to the world around you? Perhaps by planting a garden, preparing a meal with seasonal produce, or simply observing the stars.

Personal rituals can be as simple or elaborate as you choose. The key is that they should have personal significance. This could be lighting a candle daily as a symbol of inner light, writing gratitude lists, or setting intentions at the start of each new moon cycle.

Integrating new spiritual practices isn't always straightforward. You may face distractions, resistance, or skepticism from yourself or others. How can you address these challenges? Perhaps by adjusting the scope of practices, seeking community support, or continuously reflecting on the benefits these practices bring to your life.

The rewards of integrating spiritual practices that resonate with your beliefs are profound. They include increased peace of mind, deeper self-understanding, and a stronger connection to the universe. Reflect on the changes in your emotional and spiritual wellbeing since you began integrating these practices. What shifts have you noticed?

The journey to discovering and integrating spiritual practices that resonate with you is deeply personal and incredibly rewarding. It's about more than just following rituals; it's about creating a spiritual dialogue between your inner world and the external practices that you adopt. As you continue to explore and refine your spiritual practices, remember that each step on this path is an opportunity for growth, reflection, and deeper harmony with the universe. What will be your next step in aligning your spiritual practices with your soul's calling?

Embracing the Evolution of Belief

Have you ever looked back on your life and noticed how your beliefs and practices have shifted over the years? Unlike static entities, spirituality is dynamic and often evolves in response to life's changing circumstances and deepening understanding. This article explores the concept of evolving spirituality—how it changes, why it changes, and how to navigate these transformations. It's about recognizing that changes in belief are not signs of instability but markers of growth and deepening wisdom.

Spiritual beliefs can change for many reasons: personal experiences, new relationships, crises, or profound life events like birth, death, and love. Each of these can prompt questions that challenge old beliefs and encourage new perspectives. Have you ever had an experience that profoundly changed your view on life and, consequently, your spiritual beliefs?

Consider a person who grew up in a strictly religious household but finds themselves exploring other spiritual paths as they meet diverse people and encounter different cultures. Another example might be someone who turns to spirituality for the first time in the face of a personal crisis, finding comfort in practices and beliefs previously unexplored. These stories are common in the tapestry of human experience and highlight the natural evolution of our spiritual journeys.

The first step in navigating any change is embracing openness and curiosity. This means being willing to ask questions, seek answers, and be comfortable with uncertainty. How can you cultivate an open mindset towards your evolving spiritual beliefs? Practices such as meditation, reflective writing, and dialogues with others can foster this openness.

Finding a community supporting your growth can be invaluable as beliefs evolve. This might mean expanding your social circles to include people from various spiritual backgrounds or finding new spiritual or religious communities that align more closely with your changing views. How do these communities influence your spiritual evolution, and what can they offer during times of transition?

Just as we periodically assess our career paths and personal goals, reflecting on our spiritual beliefs and practices is beneficial. This could involve taking time each year to contemplate what beliefs still resonate with you and what practices genuinely enrich your life. What rituals or beliefs have become more meaningful to you over the past year? Which ones no longer serve you?

As your beliefs shift, so too might your spiritual practices. This adaptation is a healthy part of spiritual growth. It might mean altering how you pray, the type of meditation you practice, or the rituals you participate in. How have your spiritual practices evolved to better align with your current beliefs?

Navigating changes in spiritual beliefs is not just about managing doubts or uncertainties—it's about actively engaging with them to foster deeper understanding and connection. It requires flexibility, openness, and a compassionate acceptance of one's evolving self. As you continue to walk your spiritual path, remember that each phase of belief is a step towards greater self-realization and wisdom. What will be your next step in embracing the ever-changing landscape of your spirituality?

In this journey, let us be kind to ourselves and others, recognizing that spiritual growth is a continuous, life-long process that enriches our lives and those around us. How will you approach the next phase of your spiritual evolution?

A Guide to Creating a Personal Spiritual Plan

Embarking on a journey of spiritual exploration is a deeply personal and rewarding endeavor. Just as we set goals for our careers, relationships, and physical health, it's essential to have a structured plan for our spiritual development. This article will explore the steps to creating a personal spiritual plan—a roadmap to deepen your spiritual identity and find greater fulfilment on your path.

Step 1: Setting Spiritual Goals

Begin by reflecting on what you hope to achieve through your spiritual journey. Are you seeking inner peace, a deeper connection to the divine, or a greater sense of purpose? Take time to contemplate your intentions and write down your spiritual goals. These might include specific milestones you wish to reach or qualities you aim to cultivate within yourself.

Example: *Goal:* Cultivate a daily meditation practice to foster inner calm and clarity. *Goal:* Engage in acts of service to cultivate compassion and empathy towards others.

Step 2: Choosing Supportive Practices

With your goals in mind, explore different spiritual practices that resonate with you. These could include meditation, prayer, journaling, yoga, or engaging in nature. Consider which practices align with your intentions and feel meaningful to you. Remember that there is no one-size-fits-all approach to spirituality—choose practices that nourish your soul and bring you closer to your spiritual aspirations.

Example: If your goal is to cultivate mindfulness, you might incorporate a daily meditation practice into your routine. Alternatively, if you seek a deeper connection to nature, you might commit to spending time outdoors each week in contemplation and gratitude.

Step 3: Measuring Personal Growth

Reflect on your progress and growth as you engage in your chosen spiritual practices. Keep a journal to document your experiences, insights, and challenges along the way. Set regular checkpoints to review your spiritual journey and assess how your practices support your goals. Celebrate your achievements and be gentle with yourself during times of struggle.

Example: At the end of each week, set aside time to review your journal entries and reflect on any shifts in your awareness or perspective. Notice any patterns or themes emerging and consider how you can adjust your practices to better align with your evolving needs.

Creating a personal spiritual plan is an empowering step towards deepening your connection to yourself and the world around you. By setting clear intentions, choosing supportive practices, and measuring your progress, you can cultivate a more meaningful and fulfilling spiritual life. Remember that your spiritual journey is unique to you—embrace the process, trust in your inner wisdom, and allow yourself to evolve organically. As you continue on your path, may you find joy, peace, and profound spiritual growth.

Chapter 12: Integrating Spirituality into Everyday Life

In the bustling cacophony of modern life, finding solace and spiritual fulfilment can seem like an elusive quest. Yet, amidst the chaos, there are simple practices one can integrate into their daily routine to cultivate a profound sense of inner peace and purpose. Let's embark on a journey to explore these practical tips for living a spiritually fulfilling life.

As the first light of dawn breaks through the horizon, we are presented with an opportunity to set the tone for the day ahead. Morning rituals serve as anchors, grounding us in purpose and intention. Whether it's through the serenity of meditation, the solace of prayer, or the introspection of journaling, these practices create a sacred space for self-reflection and connection with the divine. By dedicating even a few moments each morning to these rituals, we pave the way for a day infused with clarity, gratitude, and inner harmony.

In the hustle and bustle of modern life, it's all too easy to get swept away by the currents of our thoughts and emotions. Mindful awareness offers a lifeline, guiding us back to the present moment with gentle grace. By cultivating a non-judgmental awareness of our thoughts, emotions, and sensations, we foster a deeper connection with ourselves and the world around us. Through this practice, we learn to savour life's simple pleasures, find beauty in the ordinary, and navigate challenges with greater resilience and equanimity.

In a world that often fixates on what's lacking, cultivating an attitude of gratitude becomes a revolutionary act. Gratitude is the gateway to abundance, inviting us to recognise and appreciate the countless blessings that enrich our lives. Whether it's the warmth of the morning sun, the laughter of loved ones, or the gift of a new day, there is always something to be grateful for. By keeping a gratitude journal or engaging in gratitude meditation, we shift our focus from scarcity to abundance, nurturing a sense of contentment and joy that radiates from within.

At the heart of spiritual fulfilment lies the spirit of service and generosity. Acts of kindness, no matter how small, have the power to ripple outward, touching the lives of others in profound ways. Whether it's volunteering at a local shelter, lending a listening ear to a friend in need, or simply offering a smile to a stranger, each act of service is a testament to our shared humanity. By cultivating compassion and empathy towards others, we contribute to our communities' well-being and deepen our sense of purpose and connection with the world around us.

Intentions serve as guiding stars, illuminating the path towards our deepest desires and aspirations. We align our actions with our core values and aspirations by setting clear intentions for how we want to show up in the world. Whether cultivating compassion, fostering creativity, or living authentically, intentions provide a roadmap for navigating life's twists and turns with grace and clarity. Through the power of intention, we empower ourselves to live with purpose and integrity, making each moment reflect our deepest truths.

Incorporating these practical tips into our daily lives offers a roadmap for living a spiritually fulfilling life. By nurturing our inner landscape with intention and mindfulness, we embark on a journey of self-discovery and transformation that enriches our lives and those around us. As we embrace these practices with an open heart and a spirit of curiosity, may we find ourselves walking a path illuminated by the light of our own inner wisdom and truth.

Navigating the Material and Spiritual World

In the hustle and bustle of modern life, it's all too easy to become ensnared in the pursuit of material wealth and external validation, often at the expense of our spiritual well-being. Yet, finding harmony between the material and spiritual worlds is essential for cultivating holistic well-being and inner peace. Here's how to navigate this delicate balance with grace and intention:

The clarity of knowing what truly matters is at the heart of finding balance. Encourage readers to embark on a journey of self-reflection, exploring their values and priorities to discern where they may be placing undue emphasis on material pursuits. By taking stock of their aspirations and desires, individuals can begin to realign their actions with their deepest values, forging a path towards greater authenticity and fulfilment.

The concept of detachment lies at the core of many spiritual traditions, advocating for a release of attachment to material possessions and external outcomes. Invite readers to cultivate a mindset of non-attachment, recognising that true happiness and fulfilment stem not from the accumulation of wealth or status, but from an inner state of contentment and peace. By relinquishing the grip of materialism, individuals open themselves to a profound sense of freedom and inner abundance.

Advocating for a simpler lifestyle may seem counterintuitive in a world that often equates success with excess. However, simplicity lies at the heart of spiritual growth, creating space for deeper connections and meaningful experiences. Encourage readers to declutter their physical and mental lives by streamlining possessions and commitments. By embracing minimalism, individuals can cultivate a sense of clarity and focus, allowing them to channel their energy towards pursuits that nourish the soul.

Financial decisions play a significant role in shaping our lives and can profoundly impact our spiritual journey. Advocate for responsible financial practices that align with spiritual values, such as mindful spending, saving, and investing. Encourage readers to view money not as an end but as a tool for creating a life aligned with their deepest aspirations. By practising financial mindfulness, individuals can cultivate a sense of abundance and security, freeing themselves from the shackles of consumerism.

Finding balance between the material and spiritual realms is not about forsaking one for the other but rather integrating the two in a harmonious way. Emphasise that material success and spiritual growth are not mutually exclusive but can coexist when approached with mindfulness and intention. Encourage readers to infuse spirituality into every aspect of their lives, from work and relationships to leisure and personal growth. By embracing this holistic approach, individuals can create a life of purpose, meaning, and profound fulfilment.

As individuals embark on the journey of balancing the material and spiritual worlds, may they find solace in the knowledge that true abundance lies not in the accumulation of wealth but in the richness of the soul. With intentionality and mindfulness, may they navigate this delicate dance with grace and find harmony in the interconnectedness of all things.

The Art of Cultivating Mindfulness in Daily Activities

Finding moments of stillness and presence can feel like a distant dream in the fast-paced whirlwind of modern life. Yet, amidst the chaos, lies the profound practice of mindfulness—a gentle invitation to anchor ourselves in the present moment and savour the richness of life's tapestry. In this exploration, we delve into the transformative power of cultivating mindfulness in our daily activities, uncovering practical techniques to infuse every moment with awareness, intention, and grace.

At its core, mindfulness invites us to shift our attention from the ceaseless chatter of the mind to the vivid tapestry of the present moment. It is a practice of non-judgmental awareness, allowing us to fully engage with the richness of our experiences without getting swept away by the currents of past regrets or future anxieties. Through mindfulness, we awaken to the beauty of life unfolding in the here and now, finding solace in the simple act of being.

From the first sip of morning tea to the gentle rhythm of our footsteps, every moment offers an opportunity to cultivate mindfulness. Encourage readers to infuse mindfulness into their daily rituals, whether it's savouring each bite of a meal, relishing the sensation of warm water cascading over skin during a shower, or simply pausing to observe the world with childlike wonder. By approaching routine tasks with intention and presence, individuals can uncover a profound sense of peace and vitality in the ordinary.

In the bustling realm of work, mindfulness serves as a guiding light amidst the chaos. Invite readers to integrate mindfulness into their professional lives by incorporating brief moments of stillness and reflection throughout the day. Encourage them to practice mindful breathing during meetings, take short walking breaks to reconnect with nature, and approach tasks with a sense of focused attention and ease. By weaving mindfulness into the fabric of their workday, individuals can enhance productivity, creativity, and overall well-being.

Physical movement provides a gateway to embodied presence, inviting us to unite mind, body, and spirit in harmonious motion. Encourage readers to explore mindful movement practices such as yoga, tai chi, or mindful walking, allowing them to cultivate a deeper connection to their bodies and the world around them. Through mindful movement, individuals can tap into a reservoir of inner peace and vitality, flowing effortlessly with the rhythms of life.

As individuals cultivate mindfulness in their daily activities, they enhance their well-being and ripple positive effects into the world around them. Mindfulness fosters greater emotional resilience, reducing stress and anxiety while promoting a profound sense of inner calm. Additionally, it deepens our connection to others, fostering empathy, compassion, and authentic communication. By nurturing mindfulness within ourselves, we become beacons of light, illuminating the path towards greater peace, joy, and spiritual fulfilment for all.

In the gentle embrace of mindfulness, may we find refuge amidst life's ebb and flow, anchoring ourselves in the present moment with grace and gratitude. By being fully present, we may uncover the boundless beauty that resides within and around us, awakening to the sacredness of each passing moment.

Nurturing Spiritual Relationships

In the intricate tapestry of human existence, relationships serve as the threads that weave together the fabric of our lives, imbuing it with meaning, depth, and richness. Yet, amidst the hustle and bustle of modern life, it's easy to overlook the profound importance of fostering spiritual connections with others. In this exploration, we delve into the transformative power of nurturing spiritual relationships, uncovering strategies to cultivate bonds that nourish the soul and ignite the spirit.

The shared heartbeat of sacred practices and rituals is at the core of spiritual relationships. Encourage readers to explore meaningful rituals with loved ones, whether it's engaging in prayer circles, meditation groups, or communal ceremonies. These shared experiences deepen bonds and create spaces for collective healing, transformation, and spiritual growth. Through shared practices, individuals find solace in the interconnectedness of their souls, forging bonds that transcend time and space.

In the sacred dance of spiritual relationships, meaningful conversations serve as the melody that resonates within the hearts of kindred spirits. Encourage readers to engage in soulful dialogues with loved ones, exploring the depths of their beliefs, experiences, and aspirations. Advocate for the practice of deep listening, wherein individuals honour each other's truths with openness, empathy, and compassion. Through meaningful conversations, individuals cultivate intimacy, understanding, and shared wisdom, enriching their spiritual journey with the gift of authentic connection.

In the tapestry of spiritual relationships, acts of kindness serve as sacred offerings of love and compassion, weaving threads of light into the lives of others. Encourage readers to perform random acts of kindness for loved ones and strangers alike, whether it's offering a listening ear, extending a helping hand, or simply sharing a smile. These acts of kindness deepen bonds and nourish the soul, fostering a sense of interconnectedness and belonging within the human family. Individuals become vessels of divine love through acts of kindness, illuminating the path towards greater compassion and unity.

In the sanctuary of spiritual community, individuals find solace in the embrace of kindred spirits, who walk alongside them on the journey of the soul. Encourage readers to seek out spiritual communities and support networks that resonate with their beliefs and values. Whether it's joining a local meditation group, attending spiritual retreats, or participating in online forums, these communities provide a sacred space for support, inspiration, and accountability in one's spiritual growth. Through the power of community, individuals discover that they are never alone on the path, finding strength in their fellow travellers' collective wisdom and love.

In the gentle embrace of spiritual relationships, may we find refuge amidst life's storms, anchoring ourselves in the sacred bonds of love, connection, and shared purpose. Through the art of nurturing spiritual relationships, may we awaken to the boundless beauty of the human spirit, walking hand in hand towards a world illuminated by the light of love and compassion.

About the Author

Elena Ray is a dedicated student of spiritual studies whose journey into the depths of various spiritual traditions has transformed her life and career as an author. With an insatiable curiosity for the world's rich tapestry of spiritual practices, Elena has travelled extensively, engaging with diverse cultures and participating in sacred rituals that have deepened her understanding of the universal quest for meaning.

Through her work, Elena aims to illuminate the profound impact of spiritual exploration on personal growth and well-being. Her insightful analysis and heartfelt narratives invite readers to consider the transformative potential of embracing spirituality.

Milton Keynes UK
Ingram Content Group UK Ltd.
UKHW020751130524
442628UK00001B/109

9 789358 811896